The
Joy of
WORSHIPING
TOGETHER

The Joy of WORSHIPING TOGETHER

Fr. Rod Damico

Resurrection Press
An Imprint of
CATHOLIC BOOK PUBLISHING CO.
Totowa • New Jersey

First published in September, 2002 by

    Catholic Book Publishing/Resurrection Press
    77 West End Road
    Totowa, NJ 07512

Copyright © 2002 by Rod Damico

ISBN 1-878718-74-6

Library of Congress Catalog Number: 2002107215

Scripture quotations are from the New Revised Standard Version of the Bible, copyright 1989 by the Division of Christian Education of the National Council of the Churches of Christ in the USA. Used by permission. All rights reserved.

Cover design and photo by John Murello

Printed in the United States.

1 2 3 4 5 6 7 8 9

DEDICATION

This book is dedicated to the people of St. Mary's Parish in Marion, Ohio, who have taught me so much about the joy of worshiping together.

ACKNOWLEDGMENTS

If I only knew. . . . Sentences that begin this way usually end with some sour sentiment. But not this time. When I reflect upon the process of preparing *The Joy of Worshiping Together,* I find that this often ominous sentence starter moves to a most happy ending. At the outset of this project, if I only knew that my family would be so supportive, if I only knew that my editor Emilie Cerar would be so helpful, if I only knew that Sr. Rene Simonelic would be so happy to provide questions and resources for the end of each chapter, and if I only knew that Dolores Leckey would prepare such a kind and insightful foreword—why I would have been singing and whistling just like the seven dwarfs when they started off to work.

I know now, and I am grateful to them all.

Contents

Foreword

The Joy of Worshiping Together creates a most graceful bridge between two authentic expressions of Church: the domestic church (the church of the home) and the gathered church (the parish). This is a much needed bridge, one long awaited in the post-Conciliar years, and traversing this bridge leads one to a richer understanding of the worshiping community. More than that, it leads one deeper into the Mystery of God.

The author, Father Rod Damico, is well suited to the task. As one of the few married Roman Catholic priests, he understands the dynamics and rituals of family life, and how they affect the people who gather Sunday mornings to celebrate the Lord's Day.

As he thinks about and reflects upon his own family—wife, children at home, and those away from home—he is able to enter into the burdens and the joys of those he will lead in worship. He understands the stress of rousing teenagers for Mass, of getting small children dressed for the occasion, of taking an urgent phone call at the last minute. More than that—he appreciates the physical, spiritual, emotional, and mental crosses people carry with them to the gathered community. And then there are the joys, the ordinary joys of family life, the celebrations which invariably take place around a meal and which are so precious to us. All of this experience is kneaded into the dough of life, the life that will be shared during worship.

Father Damico skillfully helps us to make the connections and to move from the threshold of home to that of parish church. The result? An enriched understanding of the Body of Christ and the depths of community, whether that be formed in blood or in baptism. For the single person, living alone, this means insertion into the parish family can be real and palpable. The author is convinced that no Christian need be alone and solitary, and he evokes belief in his conviction.

These are not the only connections recognized by this gifted priest. He reminds the reader of something we know, but rarely avert to, namely that invisible worshipers, angels and saints join us for what the author calls a Grand Event—the party of all parties, so to speak. One senses that his spirit is attuned to this Cloud of Witnesses (Heb 12:1) and he quietly encourages the reader to try out this spiritual sight as well, and to notice "the full house" at liturgy.

Father Damico makes yet another important connection. He clearly is well acquainted with biblical scholarship and history, and this creates yet another bridge in this engaging narrative. It is a bridge of time, connecting us to our Judaic roots and to Christian eras that gave birth to so many rituals now firmly established in our worship. As our understanding takes form, deeper love of God and one another is made possible. Finally, the author connects the joyful worship experience with pastoral care for the world. The church doors open outward, calling the laity to make the wider community a place of beatitude.

This small, elegant book offers something to Catholic Christians at different stages of life. New Catholics will learn about the meaning of worship (why we do what we do). Long-time Catholics will be reminded and refreshed regarding the centrality of worship in our lives. Spiritual seekers will glimpse a soul grown deep as the author unfolds his own joyful appreciation of Christ's living presence in the community at worship.

Dolores Leckey
Woodstock Theological Center

Introduction

"Heigh-ho, Heigh-ho, it's off to work we go!" These words, along with the catchy tune to which they were sung, still ring in my mind. So does the image of seven very different individuals joyfully heading off to work. Of course, they were not your average, run of the mill people. They were dwarfs—characters in the Disney movie *Snow White*. Even as a child, I knew this was a story, a fairy tale. I realized that I wasn't likely to run into any dwarfs in my lifetime. Yet, as I watched these lovable characters frolicking on their way to work, I did assume that they represented something I would encounter. In my youthful naiveté, I could picture people everywhere heading off to work with a smile on their face and a spring in their step. If not singing, at least they would be humming a happy tune. Incurably romantic, with an unwaveringly positive attitude, I imagined that going to work was a regular occasion for joy in human life.

It wasn't until I moved out from the bubble of my blissful childhood that I realized that going to work is not always an experience of joyful anticipation. I discovered that many people actually dread going off to work. They do not find anything exciting about their work. They do not like the people for whom they work or with whom they work. And except on paydays, they would much rather be doing something other than going to work. Rather than, "Heigh-ho," the words that usually accompany their thoughts of heading off to work are, "Oh no!"

Unfortunately, this less than enthusiastic approach to work can be seen among many Christians when it comes to the Sunday liturgy. The truth is that many Christians don't even realize that this is their work. However, the word "liturgy" means, "work of the people." Actually, celebrating the liturgy is *the* work of God's people, their most important work. This is why Christians are expected to show up each Sunday at the appointed hour. And many of them do. But often it is not with the joyful anticipation that typified the approach to work taken by the seven dwarfs. Rather, one gets the impression that if it weren't for the threat of hell or the promise of heaven, many Christians would give up this work altogether. In fact, many have.

Yet, the liturgy is intended to be a joyful work. In fact, it is meant to be the most joyful of all works. That is why we speak of "celebrating" the liturgy. The Church intends that Christians head off for worship on Sundays singing a happy song, just like the seven dwarfs. What is it that so many of us are missing? Perhaps when it comes to finding joy in our work, there is something to be learned from those dwarfs.

What were those little guys so happy about anyway? Conveniently, the reason for their joy is revealed in the song they sang as they went about their work.

> *We dig, dig, dig, dig, dig, dig, dig in our mine the whole day through*

To dig, dig, dig, dig, dig, dig, dig is what we really
   like to do
It ain't no trick to get rich quick
If you dig, dig, dig with a shovel or a pick
In a mine! In a mine! In a mine! In a mine!
Where a million diamonds shine!

The seven dwarfs were happy about going to work because they knew that it was making them rich! This is why they whistled and sang joyfully on the way to work, during work, and coming home from work. To do work that both enriches and is enriching—what could be more joyful?

Any of us who have been in a work situation like this can understand why the seven dwarfs were so happy going off to work. Several years ago I did a teaching stint at the Josephinum. I was teaching courses in homiletics and spirituality. I realized how important this work was, and I worked hard at it. But often, as I sat in my office considering how best to communicate something significant about the ministry of preaching, or, as I was caught up in the beauty of a passage from one of the spiritual classics I would be discussing with my students, I found myself smiling and saying, "I can't believe I'm getting paid to do this!" Sure I worked hard to provide a valuable service. I was enriching the lives of students, who would go on to enrich the lives of others with what I was able to give them. Yet I always felt that the riches I received were infinitely greater than the services rendered. So I often found myself singing a happy tune while I worked, just like the seven dwarfs. Like them, I worked hard to provide gems for God's people. And the work was making me rich! What could be more wonderful? Such a work situation is a true joy. And this is exactly the work situation we find ourselves in as those called to celebrate the liturgy!

In a wonderful way, the gathering of the Church for worship on Sundays enriches the life of the world. As people stream into the church on the Lord's Day, a clear message is proclaimed to all who are aware of this holy happening. God is real. God is alive. God invites all people to enter into a relationship with him. He invites them to come to him and to receive his gifts of abundant, eternal life. Gathering to worship on Sunday, the people of God testify to the most amazing thing imaginable: Though all have fallen far short of the glory of God, God has offered us salvation through Jesus Christ.

Moreover, in the gathering of Christians to celebrate the liturgy, the God to whom we bear witness actually becomes present. Through Christ, God has promised that "where two or three are gathered in my name, I am there among them" (Mt 18:20). In the fulfilling of this promise, the community where this celebration takes place is greatly enriched. For wherever the God of life is present blessings flow.

And the blessings increase as the Church does its work of praise and prayer. In union with Christ, the Church intercedes for the world's needs. It asks God's help in overcoming everything that threatens or diminishes life. This prayer is made with the promise that whatever is asked in the name of Jesus will be given (Mk 11:24). So as the Church engages in the work of prayer, God's blessings are poured out in gracious response, enriching the world in many mysterious ways.

In addition to these immediate blessings, we who celebrate the liturgy are given precious gifts that will enable us to enrich the world even more. Words of life are imparted to each one that can be used to bring joy and peace into the lives of others. The Body and Blood of Christ are fed to us, making us vessels of Christ's healing and transforming love. To have even the slightest sense of how much the liturgy contributes to the good of people everywhere should be enough to fill us with immense joy.

Add to this the many ways in which we who carry out this holy work are enriched as individuals and as a community of faith should make the joy of the seven dwarfs somber in comparison! While God's presence in our gathering blesses the entire world, it blesses us even more. That the One who is the source and end of all life takes such a personal interest in us provides an unshakable foundation for our hope and joy. But there is more. If God is present in the gathering of his people, then so are those who now dwell in God's presence. Gathering in God's company, we also gather in the company of the angels and saints. And in the gathering of those who have come to share life in Christ we are strengthened by the obvious truth that we are not alone. This is of immense value to all who struggle to hold fast to the faith.

Furthermore, as we celebrate the liturgy, we are enriched by the gifts of those who minister. Those who share their gift of song open us to the beauty of the divine reality that surrounds and enfolds us. Those who make powerful proclamations stir our hearts, creating holy longings. Those who serve with smiling faces and gracious gestures fill us with the sense that we are loved deeply and infinitely. We become the recipients of many gifts from our brothers and sisters in Christ as we celebrate the liturgy. And we are much the richer for it.

Yet it is the gifts we receive from God that enrich us the most. As we give ourselves to the work of worship, God gives us treasures of inestimable value. He imparts to us his Word, the Word that brought the universe into being, the Word that became flesh and dwelt among us, the Word that drove out demons and healed the sick, the Word that stilled the winds and seas, the Word that will save all who embrace it. This word is given to illumine, inspire, calm, and renew us. And if this were not enough of a treasure to bestow upon his people, God imparts his very life to us in the most complete and intimate of ways. God shares his gifts of bread and wine transformed into the Body and Blood of Christ. This most precious of all gifts heals and strengthens us. It gives us the nourishment we need to persevere on our difficult journey to that place where life is full and eternal. To have even the slightest sense of what it is that we receive when we celebrate the liturgy should fill us with so much joy that even the thought of it will put a song in our hearts and a spring in our steps.

This book is intended to help those who participate in the Church's worship to experience this joy. To this end I will present reflections on each part of the Sunday liturgy. I will discuss the work we do as a worshiping community in a way that brings into focus the meaning behind our actions. I will dig, dig, dig, dig, dig, dig, dig in order to uncover those gems that are the cause for joy. I will then make concrete suggestions about what we can do to enter into this joy more fully. In this way I hope to further the renewal of the worshiping community envisioned in *The Constitution on the Sacred Liturgy* of the Second Vatican Council:

> From the liturgy, therefore, and especially from the Eucharist, grace is poured forth upon us as from a fountain, and the sanctification of men in Christ and the glorification of God . . . are achieved with maximum effectiveness. (10)
>
> But in order that the liturgy may be able to produce its full effects, it is necessary that the faithful come to it with proper dispositions, that their minds be attuned to their voices, and that they

cooperate with heavenly grace, lest they receive it in vain. (11)

To know how the liturgy enriches the world and those of us who celebrate it and to be prepared to receive those benefits in full is to know the joy of being a worshiping community.

Chapter 1

THE JOY OF WORSHIPING TOGETHER

MY fifth grade teacher, Mrs. Silver, tenaciously taught those under her tutelage that to give a meaningful account of an event one must consider the Five W's: who, what, when, where, and why. Her advice has served me well over the years. In analyzing the significance of important events the Five W's usually do provide the keys to understanding. This is certainly true when it comes to understanding the most important of all events—the liturgy. The joy of this gathering is to be found in the who, what, when, where and why of it. And while any of the Five W's could be used as an access point, perhaps it is best to start with the *when*.

On the Lord's Day

Gathering time is what the biblical writers would identify as *kairos*, that is, a particular time, a time that is laden with significance. We gather on a particular day because on that day some extraordinary thing *happened*, like a birth or a marriage, the gaining of a

nation's independence or the founding of an organiza-
tion. Or we gather at a particular time because something *is happening* that we deem important, like a
funeral or an induction into some important office, or
a competition that involves those to whom we have
some special connection. When something of great
importance to us happens, time is transformed. We
step out of our usual keeping of time and enter into a
time that is extraordinary because of the meaning
attached to it. This is the kind of time that brings people together. And it is in such *meaning-full* time that
we gather for the liturgy.

Pope John Paul II provides a beautiful summary of
the significance of the time for this gathering in his
apostolic letter *Dies Domini,* ("The Day of the Lord").
In his opening paragraph he writes:

The Lord's Day—as Sunday was called from
apostolic times—has always been accorded special attention in the history of the church
because of its close connection with the very
core of the Christian mystery. In fact, in the
weekly reckoning of time Sunday recalls the day
of Christ's resurrection. It is Easter which
returns week by week, celebrating Christ's victory over sin and death, the fulfillment in him of
the first creation and the dawn of "the new creation" (cf.2 Cor. 5:17). It is the day which recalls
in grateful adoration the world's first day and
looks forward in active hope to "the last day,"

when Christ will come in glory (cf. Acts 1:11;
1 Thes. 4:13-17), and all things will be made new
(cf. Rv. 21:5). (1)

Clearly, the *when* of the Church's gathering for
liturgy is no accident. The first day of the week is also
the first day of creation. It is the day that God first said,
"Let there be . . ." and there was. This is a day of joy
because it was on this day that our lives and the lives
of everyone and everything we love became possible.
In itself, this makes Sunday an appropriate day for a
gathering of God's people.

But there is more. The day of creation is also the
day of new creation. While the gift of creation was
something wondrous indeed, it was not always treated
as such. From the beginning, people made choices
that broke their relationship with the Creator and
fatally wounded creation itself. The Scriptures provide
a long and detailed account of this devastating disinte-
gration that ensured the demise of all that God had
made. The Psalmist expresses powerfully the plight of
God's people: "If the Lord were not to help me, I would
soon go down into the silence" (94:17, *The Grail*).

Through the misuse of our God-given freedom,
humankind, along with all of creation, was heading
back into the eternal silence of nonexistence. Only
God could save us. Only God could restore his dying
creation. And it is the belief of Christians that this is
precisely what God has done through the death and
resurrection of his Son, Jesus Christ. We believe that

in Christ, God came to share life with us in time, that we might share life with him for all eternity.

In Christ, God broke the stranglehold that sin and death had gained over creation. This happened when the crucified Christ came forth from the tomb alive on Easter Sunday. This day marks the beginning of the restoring of creation, of the new creation. Christ conquered death as he said he would. And he promised that all who believe in him will share in this victory. Says St. Paul, "So if anyone is in Christ, there is a new creation: everything old has passed away; see, everything has become new!" (2 Cor 5:17).

So Sunday not only marks the dawning of creation, but also the breaking forth of the new creation. This is why, along with its distinction as the first day, Sunday is also called the eighth day. And this is precisely how *The Constitution on the Sacred Liturgy* identifies the *when* of the Church's gathering: "By a tradition handed down from the apostles and having its origin from the very day of Christ's resurrection; the Church celebrates the paschal mystery every eighth day" (106). Why the eighth day? Because with the resurrection a new day has dawned that holds forth even greater possibilities than did the first day of creation. While the first day simply made life in this world possible, the day of Christ's resurrection opened up for us the possibility of eternal life in heaven.

Knowing the *when* of our gathering for liturgy creates in us a sense of awe, wonder, and deepest joy. It provides all the inspiration we need for moving out of our daily routines to come together with others who understand the significance of Sunday. And this inspiration quickly grows into jubilation when we consider *where* this gathering takes place.

In the Lord's House

I remember the thrill I experienced as a child when my father and I went to Cleveland Municipal Stadium—the home of the Cleveland Indians. As a child growing up in the Cleveland area and a lover of baseball, the Indians were my heroes. I could imagine nothing more wonderful than being where they were. Many others shared my enthusiasm and thousands of people regularly converged on the stadium from all directions. The atmosphere was charged with excitement and festivity as people approached the gates. After all, our beloved Indians were there.

Now if people can be so thrilled about going to the house of their favorite sports team, what should our experience be when going to the house of the Lord? The Lord is the source and sustainer of all that we enjoy in life. He is the one who made the Cleveland Indians possible. And there is plenty more where that came from! Our God is absolutely awesome. And this absolutely awesome God has extended an open invitation to come to his house!

Perhaps, because God's presence extends throughout the universe we don't think of him as having a house. Yet, God has always had a place of "residence" among his people. This is not because God needs a house, but because we need him to have a house. As embodied beings, we are used to relating presence to places. For our sake, God has attached his presence to certain places. He has designated certain places as "holy," that is, as places where his presence is concentrated and where we are certain to encounter him. During the time of the Exodus, when his people were continually on the move, this special place was the tabernacle or "tent of meeting." When the people settled in the Promised Land, it was the temple in Jerusalem. Since the destruction of the temple, among the followers of Jesus, it is to those buildings dedicated as gathering places for the worshiping community that God has attached his presence in a special way.

To have even the slightest sense of the significance of such holy places is to understand the excitement expressed by the Psalmist, "I was glad when they said to me, 'Let us go to the house of the Lord!'" (Ps 122:1). How can we not be filled with wonder and deepest joy when we come to gather in the Lord's house? For the greatest and most loving of all beings has promised to meet us there. Knowing the *where* of this gathering cannot help but lead to a consideration of *who* it is that gathers in this place.

In the Presence of the Living God

> O send out your light and your truth;
>   let them lead me;
> let them bring me to your holy hill
>   and to your dwelling.
> Then I will go to the altar of God,
>   to God my exceeding joy. (Ps 43:3-4)

That we have been invited to gather at the Lord's house, where he has promised to be present, ready, and waiting for us, is utterly astonishing. It is a totally unmerited gift that God makes himself available to us in this way. While God is present to us at all times and in all places, this presence inevitably has some sense of ambiguity to it. We aren't able to see or hear God. And so, like the ancient Hebrews, we sometimes find ourselves asking, "Is the Lord with us or not?" But when we come into the Lord's house, that question has already been answered. This is the place where he dwells.

To gather *in the church* is to know that we are in the presence of the living God. Though we can't see him, the signs of his presence are all around us. The altar is the most ancient and constant symbol of the Lord's presence. Among the ancient Hebrews, the altar was a place of intense engagement with the divine. It was there that sacrifices were offered. It was the altar where God received the gifts of his people and in the receiving of them affirmed his promise to be their God.

When God came among us in Christ, a new layer of meaning was added to the altar. On the night before he offered himself upon the cross for the salvation of his people, he sat at table with his disciples. There he shared bread and wine with them, telling them that this was his body and blood which would be given for them. Quite remarkably, instead of the people offering up a sacrifice to God, here God was preparing to offer up a sacrifice on their behalf. This sacrifice was accomplished upon the cross. It was a sacrifice that made it possible for his people to share life with him forever.

The altar is a stunning vortex of divine-human encounter. It is a powerful symbol of the mutual self-giving that occurs when people "come to the place where God dwells." In Christ, God has promised that wherever two or three gather in his name, he will be present in their midst (Mt 18:20). The cross that is commonly placed in the sanctuary near the altar reminds us of just how important this ongoing sharing of presence is to God—important enough to bear the agony of crucifixion. So for God's people, coming to the altar should always be a cause for joy.

Of course, in many of our church buildings we are blessed with even more than a profound symbol of God's presence. Often in the worship space is a tabernacle where the divine presence resides. The Eucharist is kept in this special "dwelling place" to ensure that Holy Communion will be available to take to the sick and to provide a focal point for prayer and adoration. So when we gather in places of worship where the tabernacle light burns, we *know* that we have come into the presence of the living God. To think that God makes himself so available to us in the place where we gather for worship is thrilling and delightful.

In *Dies Domini*, the Holy Father speaks of the significance of our Sunday gatherings in the presence of the living Lord:

> "I am with you always to the end of the age" (Mt 28:20). This promise of Christ never ceases to resound in the church as the fertile secret of her life and the wellspring of her hope. As the day of resurrection, Sunday is not only the remembrance of a past event: It is a celebration of the living presence of the risen Lord in the midst of his people" (31).

This partly answers the question of *who* is present for the Sunday gathering. And to know that God is present is a sure tip off as to *who* else is there.

In the Company of Angels and Saints

A few days ago I phoned the home of one of our parishioners. To my surprise, my son was the one who answered the phone. Actually, it wasn't too great a surprise. It was the home of one of his close friends. In fact, he has two very close friends that spend most of their free time together. Wherever you find one, you will most likely find the others. For all intents and purposes, they come as a package deal.

What is true of my son and his friends is even truer of the company that God keeps. God is never found without his *angels* and *saints*. The Psalmist says, "In the presence of the angels I will bless you. I will adore you before your holy temple" (Ps 138:1-2, *The Grail*). Why in the presence of the *angels?* Because God never goes anywhere without them! Jesus also refers to this special connection between the angelic and the divine. Speaking of his future coming he said to his disciples, "When the Son of Man comes in his glory, and all the angels with him . . ." (Mt 25:31). Paul also reflects this understanding of the company God keeps when in First Timothy he says, "In the presence of God and of Christ Jesus and of the elect angels, I warn you to keep these instructions" (1Tim 5:21). Here the angels are referred to quite matter-of-factly as belonging to the divine presence package. Where God goes, the angels go.

And so do the *saints*. In the Letter to the Hebrews, we find a stunning description of what we encounter when entering the presence of God. The author says, "But you have come to Mount Zion and to the city of the living God, the heavenly Jerusalem, and to innumerable angels in festal gathering, and to the assembly of the firstborn who are enrolled in heaven" (Heb 12:22). The writer of Revelation also speaks of the saints as being perpetually in the presence of God.

Recounting his vision of this heavenly reality John says: "After this I looked, and there was a great multitude that no one could count, from every nation, from all tribes and peoples and languages, standing before the throne and before the Lamb . . . 'These are they who have come out of the great ordeal; they have washed their robes and made them white in the blood of the Lamb. For this reason they are before the throne of God, and worship him day and night within his temple' " (Rev 7:9, 14-15). So, along with the angels, all those holy people who have passed on from this life and have entered into the presence of God are his constant companions. Where he is, they are. Wherever he goes, they accompany him.

This is the faith of the Church. This is what our hope of heaven is all about: coming to dwell eternally in the presence of God. *The Catechism of the Catholic Church* states, "to live in heaven is 'to be with Christ'" (1025). Similarly, it notes, "'heaven' refers to the saints and the 'place' of the spiritual creatures, the angels, who surround God" (326). In other words, to be in heaven is to be in the company of God and his angels. It is to be where God is. So the saints, too, are part of the divine presence package.

This means that when we gather in God's house and come into God's presence, there is always a full house, regardless of how many persons are sitting in the pews. Every time we gather in the house of God for liturgy the place is packed! For gathering with us is a vast throng of angelic beings. And there is also a company of holy souls too numerous to count. Our heroes and heroines in the faith are there, both those known to the entire Church and those known only to us. Our loved ones, who have passed on from this life into the loving embrace of God, are there. To realize that our gathering for liturgy includes such glorious and beloved partners cannot help but fill us with wonder and delight.

With Brothers and Sisters

However, the unseen throng that gathers with us does not diminish the significance of those visibly present—at least not if we recognize *who* they are. If our gathering lacks joy and excitement it can only be because we do not realize that those we meet in God's house are our brothers and sisters.

A couple of years ago, one of our parishioners made the local papers. Pauline was in her late eighties when a woman contacted her, claiming to be her sister. While researching her family background the woman had made this startling discovery. Pauline had been put up for adoption when she was an infant. She never knew she had a sister. And her sister never knew she had a sister. But, sure enough, when the records were checked, it turned out that the woman was right. She was indeed Pauline's sister. After this confirmation of her research, she made the journey of a couple thousand miles to meet Pauline. A resident in a local nursing home, Pauline was thrilled when her sister arrived. Tears of joy flowed down her cheeks as she told reporters on the scene how wonderful it was to know she had a sister.

Knowing that we are related to another in some special way usually creates such a feeling of warmth and gladness. The ties of blood and ancestry that establish bonds between us in our human families foster a kind of joyful solidarity that enriches life immensely. Even though we may be quite different in appearance, personality, or preferences, there is something about family ties that transcends all this and creates a climate of camaraderie that we enjoy.

As I write this I think of the reunion we had recently with my wife's relatives. The Russell clan converged on a campground in Colorado from all directions and distances. Some of us hadn't seen each other for many years, but we all had shared some significant moments together as family. And though such moments had often highlighted our differences as human beings, we gathered with eagerness because the ties that bound us as family were greater than the differences between us. As each new person came into the gathering place, smiles and shouts of welcome greeted them. Joy filled that place.

Whenever people intentionally gather as families, they are usually very much aware of the special bond they share. This should also be our experience as we gather on Sunday in the Lord's house. For our faith tells us that this, too, is a family gathering. We come together as the children of God and as those who have become brothers and sisters in Christ. The fact that we do not always think of one another in this way doesn't make it any less so. It simply robs us of the joy that should be ours. In his letter to the Galatians, St. Paul says:

But when the fullness of time had come, God sent his Son, born of a woman, born under the law, in order to redeem those who were under the law, so that we might receive adoption as children. And because you are children, God has sent the Spirit of his Son into your hearts crying, "Abba! Father!" (Gal 4:4-6).

Here Paul summarizes the heart of the gospel. God has chosen us to be his adopted children. In Christ, God has brought us together into a single family. Through Baptism God imparts to us the Spirit of his Son, who dwells in us and binds us together. We are born of water and the Spirit into the family of God; we have become brothers and sisters to one another.

So when we gather for liturgy in the house of the Lord, we gather with family. We gather with those who are destined to share life with us forever in the kingdom of our Heavenly Father. To view one another this way as we come together around God's altar deepens our sense of awe and wonder at the remarkable assembly of which we are a part. Yet, there is even more to our relationship with those who gather for the

Sunday liturgy than this—something more mysterious and more glorious. For those who have received the Spirit of Christ have become one body!

As the One Body of Christ

For just as the body is one and has many members and all the members of the body, though many, are one body, so it is with Christ. For in the one Spirit we were all baptized into one body— Jews or Greeks, slaves or free—and we are all made to drink of one Spirit (1Cor 12:12-13).

Sharing common human bloodlines does create strong ties between family members. But because of the mixing of bloodlines through marriage, it is not exactly the same blood that courses through the veins of each family member. In fact, different family members may not even have the same blood type. While a biological family may share life profusely, intimately, and intentionally, it can only be spoken of as a single organism metaphorically.

But those of us who have become brothers and sisters in Christ are a single body. We are *organically* connected. For we share the one Spirit of God manifested powerfully in the person of Jesus, drawing us together into a communion of love and common purpose, forming us into a single body. Together with him, we form a single functioning unit as a single living organism.

To realize this is to know something of the importance of our gathering on Sunday mornings. We gather because we belong together. This means that there is really no such thing as a solitary Christian. We cannot be the one body of Christ in isolation from one another. We can only be most fully who we are and most effectively who we are when we gather with the rest of the body.

We need each other. Perhaps it is the supportive smile of one that will quicken the heart of another; or the voice of one that will add strength to the singing, stirring everyone to greater participation; or the strength of one that will physically assist another in making their way into the Lord's house; or the mothering of one that will stir up the loving inclinations of others; or the youthful enthusiasm of one that will enliven many; or the sorrowful countenance of one that moves the community to be mindful of those who are suffering. Each member of the body has something to contribute that makes the assembly better than it would be without him or her. It was for this reason that the author of the third century church manual *The Teaching of the Twelve Apostles* wrote, "When you are teaching, command and exhort the people to be faithful to the assembly of the church. Let them not fail to attend, but let them gather faithfully together. Let no one deprive the Church by staying away; if they do, they deprive the body of Christ of one of its members!" (chapter 13).

That we are one body in Christ is cause for celebration because it means that we are never alone. We have ties with others that go beyond those of family and geography. They are ties that bind powerfully and permanently because God's Spirit is the binding agent. When we realize this we no longer see the Sunday gathering as a conglomeration of disparate people with uncommon interests—a kid with a runny nose, an old woman struggling with a walker, a mother trying to quiet her infant, an on-call doctor with pager attached to belt, a young couple holding hands, a recent widow with a tear rolling down her cheek. These people belong to us as much as our hands, feet, or heart. We belong together. It is a wondrous thing, a joyous thing to realize this.

But this joyful reality is also a challenging one because it means that we have an obligation to be present to one another. We have a duty to share our gifts and our attention with those who have become an essential part of our life through our baptism into Christ. If we withhold our presence and our gifts something will be lacking. The effectiveness of Christ's work through his body, the Church, will be compromised because we have deprived the body of one of its members. Our gathering is that important, particularly in light of *what* we gather for on the Lord's Day and *why*.

To Celebrate the Liturgy

To know the *who, when* and *where* of this gathering is also to know the *what* and the *why* of it. *Why* else would the body of Christ gather but to do *what* the body of Christ does? The Scriptures tell us that "Christ Jesus came into the world to save sinners" (1 Tim 1:15). To carry out the work of redemption, to reconcile the world to God is what Christ does. It is what Christ wants to do, loves to do, and rejoices in doing. So it is with those who have become part of the body of Christ through baptism. This is the great dignity and the endless joy of those who have been baptized into Christ and gather on the Lord's Day. We have been chosen by God to share in the most significant mission of all time and of all places. We have been chosen to participate in God's saving work. It's for this very reason that what we gather for on the Lord's Day is called "liturgy."

According to *The Catechism of the Catholic Church,* "In Christian tradition [the word "liturgy"] means the participation of the People of God in 'the work of God.' Through the liturgy Christ, our redeemer and high priest, continues the work of our redemption in, with, and through his Church" (1069). Those Christians who think they are coming to church on Sunday simply to receive a little spiritual nourishment are missing out on what is most thrilling about this gathering. It is not only those gathered who benefit. But in the coming together of the body of Christ for liturgy, *benefit is brought to the whole universe.* The celebration we share in today is paving the way for an eternity of blissful gathering in the kingdom of heaven.

This is why we speak of "celebrating" the liturgy. Knowing *what* we do when we gather as the body of Christ and *why* is to understand the meaning of these now famous words from *The Constitution on the Sacred Liturgy,* "The liturgy is the summit toward which the activity of the Church is directed; it is also the fount from which all its power flows" (10).

QUESTIONS FOR REFLECTION

1. With all the demands on our time, we tend to treat Sunday as just another day. What steps can you take to keep Sunday holy?

2. Why is "God's House" a special place?

3. Name and describe a new acquaintance that you made at a recent Sunday liturgy. How will you acknowledge your new brother or sister in Christ?

4. In what ways do you help the parish family grow in solidarity?

5. Complete the statement: If there were no Sunday Mass, I would miss the opportunity to . . .

Chapter 2

THE JOY OF GATHERING

OUR REASON FOR JOY

THE people are assembled. The musicians have been tuning their instruments for quite some time. The audience has reviewed the program. Some are engaged in quiet conversation in anticipation of what is to come. Others are silent, thinking of some of the pieces to be played. Excitement builds as the appointed time approaches. Suddenly the musical warm-up ceases. An expectant hush takes hold as a door opens and the conductor enters. As he makes his way to the conductor's stand, all present—musicians and audience together—break into spontaneous applause. Of course, the conductor knows that the applause is not primarily for him. It is mainly an expression of the people's readiness for the program to begin.

The conductor takes up his baton. Things grow still. And with a wave of his hand, the sound of a stirring melody fills the room. As the music washes over the crowd, all are taken up into it, embracing the purpose for this gathering and giving themselves over to it. By the time the piece ends, those present are focused and ready for what they have come to do. It is then that the conductor greets them and makes a few brief comments about the program that they have already entered into, so that they may have a stronger sense of its significance. He might encourage them to let go of any burdens or preoccupations that would keep them from entering into the experience fully. Perhaps he offers a word of praise for the benefactors who have made the performance possible. And he concludes his opening remarks by expressing the hope that the expectations of those gathered will be fulfilled in every way.

Many of the grand events of human life begin something like this. People come from various places for a common purpose. They come for the performance of a great symphony, an athletic competition, a rally in support of a particular cause, or some other significant event. And all have an important part to play. If those in the general assembly are not engaged with what is happening and responsive to it, the players, actors, speakers, or musicians lose much of their inspiration. And without the inspired sharing of the special gifts of the performers, the assembly won't be able to enter into the experience enthusiastically.

Since everyone's participation is important, they all must be brought together. They must be gathered. So it is no accident that most significant events in life have some brief way of gathering people, of focusing their attention, of reminding them of why they have come together, and of moving them into participation in the event itself. The Sunday liturgy is no exception.

Gathering Around God's Altar

It is not too hard to imagine what people have gone through to make it to the Lord's House at the appointed hour on the Lord's Day. In one household Tom and Maggie Johnson, who waited up for their late-arriving teens (pushing the Saturday night curfew to its outer limits), stumble out of bed groggily, realizing that they have a challenge before them: How to wake their young night owls from sleep for the most important event of the week and do it in a way that will shield the younger members of the family from the brief skirmish that may evolve. This battle won, locating the youngest child's shoes is the next challenge. Having a bite of breakfast has turned into nothing more than a passing thought as the necessary time of departure draws distressingly near. The promise of a post-Mass brunch filled with family favorites has settled the troops as they pile into the van, leaving Sam, the disappointed dog, behind.

Down the road elderly Mary Smith has been ready and waiting over an hour for the Tanners who take her to church every Sunday. This Sunday morning excursion to church is one of the few times she gets out of her house. And, as the time draws near, she is afraid that the Tanners have forgotten her. Meanwhile, the

Tanners have been talking long distance to their daughter who is suffering from depression.

In yet another house, Jack Kennard, one of the lectors, is in the basement practicing the reading he will soon be proclaiming, while his wife Julia, the cantor, is in the shower singing the psalm that will follow. And Father Peterson is in the rectory preaching to Methuselah, his cat, the homily he will soon be delivering to his congregation. He takes the cat's surprising attentiveness as an encouraging sign that the people will find his message engaging.

This is just a small representation of those who make their way into the church at the appointed hour for the celebration of the liturgy. Each Sunday, people come from all different kinds of circumstances and experiences. They need to be gathered within themselves and with the others present, who also have come to do the work of the body of Christ. They need to be gathered with the God who is present there, along with his angels and saints.

And at the appointed hour, this is what happens. The gathering begins with a *song* and a *procession*. Why a song? According to *The General Instruction on the Roman Missal*, the purpose of the Entrance Song is "to open the celebration, deepen the unity of the people, introduce them to the mystery of the season or feast, and accompany the procession" (25). The liturgy reflects a great wisdom here. One of the most effective ways of bringing people together quickly is through the singing of a song that is recognized by those assembled and expresses their reason for gathering.

And what the entrance song does audibly, the procession does visibly. The servers and the priest move through the congregation to the altar. Contrary to what is commonly thought, the procession is not a way of drawing attention to the one who is going to preside over the assembly. Rather, this movement through the people is intended to bring everyone's attention to the altar. Those who work in the field of communication tell us that movement captures attention. So the movement of those in the procession captures the attention of those assembled and directs it to where it belongs. While it is true that the priest represents Christ, the head of the body, his coming to the altar does little good unless the entire body comes with him.

The procession, then, is about the entire community gathering around the central symbol of God's presence. So when the priest *venerates the altar with a kiss* and perhaps *incenses it,* it is an action done on behalf of all God's people, who are now gathered in the presence of God. The making of *the sign of the cross,* the mark all received when they became a part of this family of faith, is the physical expression of the people's coming together as the body of Christ around God's altar. The priest's *greeting* then expresses the significance of this particular gathering of the body of Christ. *The General Instruction on the Roman Missal* articulates the purpose of the greeting

quite nicely: ". . . through a greeting the priest expresses the presence of the Lord to the assembled community. This greeting and the people's response manifest
the mystery of the Church that is gathered together"
(28). *The GIRM* also notes that the priest or other suit-
able minister may briefly introduce the Mass, identifying the particular aspect of the mystery of life in Christ
being celebrated (29). A *sprinkling rite* may follow, in
which the entire congregation quite literally gets a feel
for the reality they have entered into as the assembled
body of Christ. Most often, though, the sprinkling with
holy water is reserved for more festive occasions. More
commonly, following the greeting, those assembled
proceed directly to a rite intended to remove any
impediments to their truly being one body gathered to
do the work of Christ.

Confessing Our Sins

We all know that we cannot *really* come together
with others unless the things that have come between
us are dealt with. Many years ago, I was the coordina-
tor for a large conference in Columbus, Ohio. As people arrived and checked out the facilities, I could tell
that the accommodations weren't quite as nice as some
had expected them to be. At our initial gathering, in
order to bring the people together in a way that would
enable them to focus on what we had come to do, after
a brief word of welcome I apologized for some of the
problems with the accommodations. This honest

expression of my own disappointment and my promise to do everything I could to rectify the situation really helped to diffuse the hostility and further unite us as a people assembled for a common purpose. The truth is that confession is not only good for the soul of the one doing the confessing. It is also good for the union of souls.

In the prayer Jesus taught he included the petition, "And forgive us our trespasses, as we forgive those who trespass against us." Jesus knew that to enter that place where all God's people are gathered as one, there could be no lingering grounds for separation. So as we enter into the Kingdom through the celebration of the liturgy, we confess that we have sinned against God and against one another.

This common confession that we are sinners in need of mercy unites us deeply. As we speak and listen to others asking for God's mercy, we know we cannot withhold it from one another. The prayer voiced by the priest at the conclusion of the *penitential rite* is really the prayer of all present, "May almighty God have mercy on us, forgive us our sins, and bring us to everlasting life." The "me" and "my" of the sins we have called to mind and confessed have become the "us" and the "our" of our prayer for mercy and forgiveness. Our common confession has removed unspoken barriers separating us from one another and from God. And it creates a joy among us that is appropriately expressed in a song of praise.

And Praising the God Who Saves Us

"Glory to God in the highest, and peace to his people on earth." Those who have received the gift of peace through the penitential rite now sing these words, first sung by the angels at the announcement of the Savior's birth. It is the gift of peace, of *shalom*—the making whole of God's creation, that we have experienced in our communal act of reconciliation. Having caught this glimpse of the meaning of the "eighth day," the day of the new creation made possible by God's gift of reconciliation in Christ, how can we keep from singing? In taking up this "song of the angels," we are opened more fully to the presence of the unseen contingent of our assembly—the entire host of heaven. This song of joy, the *Gloria,* unites us with all those who gather around the throne in God's kingdom, proclaiming the praises of God. Heaven and earth join together in this eternal expression of our cause for celebration. The gathering of the worshiping community is almost complete. All that remains is to offer what has been gathered to the Father.

We Offer Our Collective Prayer

While the community now has been gathered into one for the celebration of the liturgy, it is a unity that acknowledges the importance of each one gathered. Though all have assembled for a common purpose, the life circumstances of each one present are unique.

Each member of the body has his or her particular burdens, concerns, hopes, and reasons to be thankful. So gathering the assembly into one requires taking up the stuff of each person's life and presenting it to the Father. And this is precisely what the *collect* does.

When the priest says, "Let us pray," he is inviting all present to silently offer the petitions that flow from their own lives to the Father. The priest then concludes these silent prayers with a spoken prayer that gathers them all up into a single prayer. This voiced prayer is intended to connect the prayers of all present to the particular aspect of the paschal mystery being celebrated that day. Hence, the prayer is called the *collect* from the Latin word *collecta*, meaning a gathering up or a collection. Presenting our collective prayer to the Father, who is always ready to "give good things to those who ask him" (Mt 7:11), is a most fitting and joyful way to conclude the gathering rites.

OPENING TO THE JOY

When we are preparing to go to any special event we usually do some anticipatory thinking and talking. This prepares us to enter into the experience with enthusiasm. When my daughter was preparing to go to a concert by one of her favorite groups a few weeks ago, every time I walked by her room I heard the music of that group playing. The little snippets of her phone conversations I heard were all about going to the concert. By the time the day of the concert rolled around she was filled with such joyful anticipation of the event that I'm sure she would have jogged the hundred miles to get there if the car hadn't started.

I think we have something to learn from such experiences about readying ourselves for participation in the liturgy. A little advance preparation goes a long way towards creating in us a sense of joyful anticipation. Calling to mind the *who, what, when, where,* and *why* of our gathering will help us to enter into it with a genuine spirit of openness and eagerness. So throughout the week and particularly before we leave our homes to go to Mass, it is good to spend some time reflecting on the significance of going to the *Lord's house* on the *Lord's Day* to do the *Lord's work.*

Preparing for the Gathering

We will be better prepared for participation in the Sunday liturgy if, before actually going there, we give some thought to the significance of the Lord's house for us.

- What are some of the most memorable experiences we have had in church?
- What do we like most about being in church?
- What special people are we most likely to encounter there?
- What are the particular concerns that we will be taking with us into the Lord's house this week?

- What are the things for which we want to offer thanks to the Lord?

Reflecting on these questions with family and friends or in our own quiet moments of meditation will make it much more likely that we will rejoice when they say to us, "Let us go to the house of the Lord!"

Greeting One Another Warmly

How we greet one another upon entering the church will have a profound effect on our readiness to be gathered into a unified body for the liturgy. But here again, a little advance preparation goes a long way toward making our greeting of one another a joyful experience. In this regard, we can take a few tips from the world of business. One of the basic strategies for business success is to learn as much as possible about those one hopes to engage in a common venture before actually meeting with them. What are their concerns? What are their needs? What are their gifts? What difficulties might we have relating to them? What can we do to overcome those difficulties and have a positive exchange?

So it is when it comes to meeting one another in the house of God for the business of liturgy. A little advance preparation goes a long way.

- Who are those in the congregation for whom we have developed a special affection?
- What is it that we enjoy about these individuals?

- What experiences have we shared that have created a special sense of closeness to them?

Thinking of such persons certainly increases our eagerness to share in the gathering for liturgy.

It is also helpful to spend some time thinking of those in the church community who are suffering in some way. We are likely to encounter the woman whose husband has died recently or the child whose parents have just divorced. We might be sitting near the middle-aged man who has just lost his job or the teenager who was recently in a serious car accident. Perhaps the young couple will be present whose little boy was just diagnosed with leukemia. As we think of those in our gathering who have come on hard times it is good to pray for them beforehand and to anticipate supporting them with a kind word or a warm greeting. It adds meaning to our gathering on the Lord's Day.

Quite possibly, there will be people in the assembly who do not bring an immediate feeling of joy to us when we think of them. We might have had a bad experience with someone in the past. Maybe there is something about a particular individual that we find irritating or even upsetting. It happens. There's no use denying it. In fact, when it comes to preparing ourselves to greet one another warmly in the house of God, it is essential to acknowledge that coming together with some individuals may present a bit of a challenge. Part of our reflection in preparation for the Sunday gathering should include the intentional calling to mind of such people—bringing them before the Lord in prayer, trying to see them as the Lord does, being open to their hurts and struggles, and asking the Lord to help us love them. Often such "prayer-in-advance" helps us to move beyond our resistances and greet others warmly in the Sunday assembly.

Coming Together into God's Presence

Of course, our fellow parishioners are not the only ones we will be meeting at the church on Sunday. While it is certainly important to think of them, it is only when we spend some time considering *whose* house we will be going to that we will be most fully open to the joy of gathering for liturgy.

I remember the first time I was invited to meet our bishop in his office at the chancery. He was the head of our diocesan church. I was working for him in one of his diocesan offices. Much of my spiritual and material well-being depended on him. And now I was going to meet him personally! For days before my appointment with the bishop I thought about what I should wear, what I should say, and how I should say it. I even thought about when I should leave home to get there on time.

When the day of my meeting with the bishop arrived, I was filled with such anticipation that I could hardly stand it. Showering and shaving took on much greater significance than usual. I was sure to pick out a pair of socks without holes. I shined my shoes and put on my best suit. I was filled with a sense of the importance of what I was about to do. I left home about twenty minutes earlier than necessary. And as I drove, all I could think of was what I would do when I came into the bishop's office. It was all very exciting.

Thankfully, I knew some of the people who worked in the bishop's office. The thought of being greeted by them eased my nervousness somewhat. I knew they were supportive of me. Actually we were all part of a large team doing important work. Anticipating their presence made my trek to the bishop's office all the more special.

A similar dynamic should be at work when we come to the church for the Sunday liturgy, only more so. Taking the time to reflect beforehand about the awesome privilege of coming into the Lord's house for a personal meeting with the God of all creation certainly adds a sense of wonder to our Sunday churchgoing. It will have implications for what we wear and how we conduct ourselves. Obviously, entering into God's presence is not something that should be done casually or irreverently. It is hard to imagine going to the White House to meet the president of the United States dressed in shorts and a tank top. It is hard to imagine arriving after the appointed time. And it is definitely hard to imagine carrying on in a thoughtless or disrespectful manner while in his presence. It should be even more difficult to imagine such things when it comes to a meeting with our God. But, then, this is the key: actually taking the time to imagine and to prepare.

Part of our preparation for liturgy each Sunday includes our daily turnings to the God we will meet there. Our Sunday gathering should be an exciting culmination of our encounters with God throughout the week. If we are taking the life of faith seriously we will have moments when we are filled with a sense of how awesome God is. We will be aware of God's handiwork in creation, so vast and complex. We can see the things we find delightful in life as gifts of the good God. In our reading of Scripture we may be amazed by the many ways God has worked his salvation among his people over the centuries. At times we may find ourselves pondering the depth of God's love for us as revealed in his coming among us in Christ. Then, in preparation for participating in the liturgy, we can ask ourselves: How can we most fittingly present ourselves to such an amazing God as we come to his house for worship? Surely we will find ourselves scrambling to find the best outfits in our wardrobes, putting a shine on our shoes, and cleaning ourselves up as best we can. We are going to meet our God. This is big!

Along with such reflections, we would do well to call to mind those things we will encounter in God's house that will speak to us of his unseen presence. What do the altar, ambo, cross, and tabernacle tell us about the God who has promised to be with us in this holy place? Taking the time to reflect upon the primary symbols in God's house beforehand will open us more fully to God's presence when we enter into it. So will reading the Scriptures for the liturgy beforehand (something I will discuss more fully in the next chapter).

Our sense of anticipation will be increased even more if we also take the time to think of the multitude of angels and saints who are always in God's company. If we take a few moments during the week to think of the angels who have played such an important role in the lives of God's people, and especially those angels who have been watching over us; if we spend a little time reading about the saints and remembering where their saintly lives have led them; if we prayerfully call to mind our beloved dead, whom we have commended to the Lord's presence; then we cannot help but come into the church for the Sunday liturgy filled with joyful anticipation. Having thus prepared ourselves we will enter into the singing, processing, praising, and praying as those eager to gather in the presence of God together with his angels and saints.

QUESTIONS FOR REFLECTION

1. At most concerts and sporting events, we move from being spectators to becoming participants engaged in the event. How would you describe this transition in terms of participation in the Mass?

2. Think about a time that you reached out to a member of your family or parish community with forgiveness or compassion. Identify how this coming to peace changed the way that you actively participate in the Mass?

3. Why is the Gathering Rite incomplete for you and for others if you are not present?

4. What speaks to you of God's unseen presence when the community gathers for liturgy?

5. What do you bring to the altar on Sunday from your experience of life all week long?

Chapter 3

THE JOY OF RECEIVING
A LIFE-GIVING WORD

OUR REASON FOR JOY

The gathering rites are not simply a preparatory exercise that readies us to take up the work of the liturgical assembly. This gathering together as the body of Christ in the Lord's house is actually the beginning of our work. In this coming together, we bear witness to the God who has come among us in Christ. But there is more to the work entrusted to us than this. Having borne witness to the reality of God, we now take up the vital work of proclaiming his word. To understand just how vital a work this is, perhaps it will help to revisit a remarkable story that involves the proclaiming of God's word.

As the story begins we find the prophet Ezekiel on one of those strange, mystical journeys for which he is well known. Transported by the Spirit, he had been plopped down in the middle of a valley. It was not the kind of valley Ezekiel would have chosen to visit if he had been in charge of the flight. The valley was filled with bones. And the bones were so dry that they could have crumbled into dust at any moment. It must have been a chilling sight. It was the stuff of which horror movies are made.

In the midst of this ghastly gathering of lifeless remains the Lord asked Ezekiel a question that rattled him. "Can these bones live?" Well, Ezekiel had been working with God for a long time now and could recognize a set up when he saw one. "I don't know, but I'm sure you're going to tell me," is a loose translation of his response. And he was right. Only God did more than tell him. He involved the prophet in a little object lesson that he would never forget.

The Lord commanded Ezekiel to prophesy to those bones. He was to speak God's word to a bunch of dry, lifeless bones! And this is what the prophet did. To his amazement, as he spoke the word of the Lord in this valley-turned-graveyard, things started happening. The bones started rattling and coming together to form skeletons. As he continued proclaiming God's word, flesh and skin began to cover the bones. Realizing that this was no time to stop and fortified by God's command, Ezekiel continued proclaiming the word. And before he knew it, that valley of death was filled with a throng of living, breathing people standing on their feet and carrying on as though this kind of thing happened every day.

Well, the truth of the matter is that with God, this kind of thing does happen every day. Whenever God's word is spoken, life is renewed in remarkable ways.

This little object lesson on the life-giving power of God's word given to Ezekiel has been passed on from generation to generation as one of the central tenets of the Judeo-Christian tradition. Fundamental to our faith is the belief that the God who brought creation into being through the speaking of a word, can also restore it and bring it to perfection by the power of his word. This is why the centerpiece of the Jewish synagogue service has always been the reading and interpreting of the sacred Scriptures. And it is for the very same reason that the followers of Jesus continued this practice when they established their own distinctive form of worship. Our tradition and experience affirms a truth first spoken by Moses and repeated by Jesus, "One does not live by bread alone, but by every word that comes from the mouth of God" (Dt 8:3, Mt 4:4).

In fact, the proclaiming of God's word is fundamental to our existence as the body of Christ. It is our belief that Jesus is the Word, the Word who was in the beginning with God, the Word through whom all things have come to be, and the Word that is God. Jesus is that divine Word from the Father that gives life to the world (Jn 1:1-4). Jesus is the source and fulfillment of all the life-giving words that God has spoken to his people. So, in a sense, when the body of Christ gathers, the Word is already spoken. The Word that is Christ is proclaimed in visible form.

Yet, there is richness to the word of God that goes beyond this. It touches every facet of life, addressing both the shared and individual experiences of all people, enlivening the hearts of those who receive it. The proclaiming of this word was a central aspect of Jesus' work. As the body of Christ, we carry on this work in the celebration of the liturgy—first, through the *proclaiming of the sacred Scriptures.*

The Readings Are Proclaimed

The proclaiming of the Scriptures is of great benefit to those who are willing to listen. It is for this reason that the Second Vatican Council decreed in its *Constitution on the Sacred Liturgy:* "The treasures of the Bible are to be opened up more lavishly, so a richer share in God's word may be provided for the faithful" (51). The Scriptures provide an amazing record of God's speaking to his people over the centuries. In itself, this is of great value. But there is more to the Scriptures than this. These inspired writings serve as a medium through which God speaks to us now, addressing us both personally and communally. In other words, the inspiration that began with the composition of these texts continues in their proclamation. God speaks afresh every time the Scriptures are proclaimed. And, as we know, when God speaks, things happen!

To further understand the great importance of this part of the liturgy it is helpful to read the *Introduction to the Lectionary.* This beautiful and insightful docu-

ment has this to say about the proclamation of the
readings:

> ... the word of God unceasingly calls to mind and
> extends the economy of salvation, which
> achieves its fullest expression in the Liturgy . . .
> The word of God constantly proclaimed in the
> Liturgy is always, then, a living and effective
> word through the power of the Holy Spirit. It
> expresses the Father's love that never fails in its
> effectiveness toward us. (4)
>
> Whenever, therefore, the Church, gathered for
> liturgical celebration, announces and proclaims
> the word of God, she is aware of being a new peo-
> ple in whom the covenant made in the past is per-
> fected and fulfilled. Baptism and Confirmation in
> the Spirit have made all Christ's faithful into mes-
> sengers of God's word because of the grace of
> hearing they have received. They must be the
> bearers of the same word in the Church and in
> the world . . . (7)

Here the Church makes the bold affirmation that the
proclaiming of the word extends the saving work of
Christ. And indeed it does. It extends the saving work
of Christ first by renewing and nourishing those who
make up the body of Christ.

I was blessed recently with an experience that
helped me understand something of how this is
accomplished. Gathering with a family in preparation

for a funeral Mass, I listened as they shared their remembrances of the woman who had died. Her name was Martha. Martha had been widowed for seventeen years. And through all those years, she had missed her husband Robert terribly. Their marriage had been a true union of love. During our conversation the grand-children spoke of several boxes of letters Martha had saved. They were love letters Robert had sent her during World War II. Every now and then she would pull those letters out and read them. In her last years she sometimes invited her grandchildren to join her in reading them.

The grandchildren noted that during the reading of those letters a change came over Martha. They would notice a smile or hear a sigh. They would sometimes be surprised by the sudden liveliness of her expressions and the obvious increase in her physical energy. Anyone who has ever received even one such letter understands something of this dynamic. Such affirmations of how much we matter to someone are healing and renewing, especially when that someone matters greatly to us. It frees us from the kind of negative thinking about ourselves that pulls us down and leads to destructive behavior. Also, the sharing of another's deepest thoughts and concerns with us is energizing. It renews our sense that our lives really matter and inspires us to live them well. Such sharing can instant-ly transform a valley of dry bones into a place where life is bursting forth all over.

In the proclaiming of the Scriptures we have such expressions of love and concern. To think that God regards us so highly as to communicate with us at all should be enough in and of itself to have us turning cartwheels in the aisles! What God shares with us through the Scriptures should fill us with the kind of rush of new life that Martha's grandchildren witnessed when they saw her reading those old love letters. The Scriptures are a gift of God's love and, if they are recognized as such, will bring new life to all who receive it.

And this word that enlivens also nourishes. When after forty days of fasting Jesus was tempted by the devil to turn some nearby stones into bread, Jesus responded, "Man does not live by bread alone but by every word that comes from the mouth of God" (Mt 4:4). He only could have made this response because he had found in the Scriptures a great source of nourishment. While it was true that bread was necessary to continue on in his worldly existence, Jesus recognized that the word of God provides what is necessary to grow into eternity. St. Paul expresses this same understanding of the nourishing quality of God's word in his Second Letter to Timothy. In the third chapter he reminds Timothy, "from childhood you have known the sacred writings that are able to instruct you for salvation" (3:15). In the Scriptures God provides stories, commandments, wise sayings, stirring examples, inspired songs, and instructions that nourish the mind and heart. When the readings are proclaimed in the liturgy we are given the nourishment we need to carry on the work of the body of Christ until our time for laboring is done and we come into the kingdom.

While the body of Christ is being renewed and nourished through the proclaiming of the readings, it is also being equipped. The same word that feeds and freshens us in the liturgy is the word we have to proclaim to the Church and to the world. Again and again in the Scriptures, particularly in the books of the prophets, we hear that the word of the Lord came to someone. While this word undoubtedly enriched the one who received it, the giving of the word was always attached to the rendering of some service on behalf of God's people. For instance, in the story of the prophet Jeremiah's call we are told that the word of the Lord came to him. But this word was not just for his benefit. It was given to be passed on to others. Said the Lord to Jeremiah, "Now I have put my words in your mouth. See, today I appoint you over nations and over kingdoms, to pluck up and to pull down, to destroy and to overthrow, to build and to plant" (Jer 1:9).

This is always the way it is with the word of the Lord. It is so fertile that it is bound to be of benefit to more than those who first receive it. The word proclaimed in the liturgy is both for *enriching* God's people and for *equipping* them to serve the Church and the world. We are given a word to share with others that has the power to save—a word that will convert, deliver, heal, restore, and enlighten. We can be confident of this because of the One who gives it.

God Speaks

The effectiveness of this proclaimed word is something we can count on because it is not dependent on those doing the proclaiming. Rather, its effectiveness depends on the One who is present and speaks *through* the proclaiming. We understand something about this from our common human experience. For instance, when a letter or an e-mail comes to Mary and I from one of our children, say our daughter Elizabeth, sometimes Mary will read it out loud to me. But though she is doing the reading, it is Elizabeth that I am really hearing. I can see her and even hear her voice. The reading of her words makes her present to me in a very real sense because it is her word that is being read. The Elizabeth that resides in my memories and in my heart is speaking to me.

So it is when the word of God is proclaimed. However, when it comes to the reading of God's word, the presence is more than what is produced by memory and emotion. For God's very nature is to be personally present at all times and in all places. So the gift of God's word always carries with it the gift of Godself. When the Scriptures are read, God is present. It is God who speaks to us. And thank God that it is. After all, neither the word on the page nor the person vocalizing it has the power to save us. This is something only God can do. And this is what God does do. According to the *General Instruction on the Roman Missal,* "When the scriptures are read in the Church, God himself is speaking to his people, and Christ, present in his own word, is proclaiming the Gospel"(9). Knowing this should certainly prompt us to sit up and listen when the Scriptures are being proclaimed!

The Preacher Connects

Yet there is more to the Liturgy of the Word than the proclaiming of the Scriptures. There must be. The hearing of a word has no great effect on us unless that word is appropriated. In other words, the word must be taken into the context of one's life and embraced if it is going to make a difference. Some further reflection is necessary if connections between the word and our lives are to be made. This is the purpose of the *homily.*

The homily connects the word proclaimed in the readings with the lives of the people who hear them. Such a project is definitely a challenge. During the readings, each person in the assembly may find that a particular word holds some special meaning. But because each one has his or her own unique life circumstances and concerns, that word will not be the same for everybody. So if the community is to come together around God's word, someone must intentionally work at making the connections. This is the preacher's job. In a sense, the preacher must do what the presider does in the collect at the conclusion of the

gathering rites. He must bring all the different responses to the word together by focusing them around a particular message that has meaning for the entire assembly.

In a sense, the Liturgy of the Word can be viewed as
an exercise of communal *lectio divina*—a time-honored
practice among Christians. It is a way of reading and
meditating on the word of God that enables one to
become the "good soil" described in the Parable of the
Sower. According to Jesus, becoming good soil for the
word requires us to "hold it fast in an honest and good
heart, and bear fruit with patient endurance" (Lk 8:15).
In the individual practice of *lectio divina*, this is done by
reading the Scriptures out loud, slowly and attentively,
until one comes upon a word or phrase that seems to
contain some special significance. At this point the
reading stops and one "holds fast" that word, meditating upon its meaning until there is nothing more to
draw from it. Receiving the "fruits" of this meditation,
one will be moved to offer some simple prayer in
response. Perhaps one may even be lifted into a period
of quiet contemplation. Then, if there is still time, one
takes up the reading of the Scripture again.

We do something similar in the Liturgy of the Word.
No, the readings are not stopped periodically for immediate reflection. But in the homily that follows, the
preacher does focus the congregation on various points
in the readings, or perhaps on a single point. He mulls
over something that was proclaimed in the readings in

a way that relates it to the particular mystery being celebrated in the liturgy and connects it to the lives of the people. He reflects with the people on just what this word has to do with who they are and what they do as members of the body of Christ. In this way the preacher makes it possible for the people to hang on to the word in a way that will have some good and lasting effect.

The God who is present and speaking through the proclaiming of the readings, also is present and speaking through the preaching of the homily. According to the *Introduction to the Lectionary*, "Christ himself is always present and active in the preaching of the Church" (24). It may be the preacher's words that capture the people's attention, but it is God himself who speaks to their hearts. And if the people really hear God speaking to them through the readings and the homily, they will surely be moved to respond.

The People Profess Their Faith and Pray

If people truly have a sense of being addressed by God, they cannot help but respond, "I believe!" So the communal recitation of the creed naturally follows the homily. According to the *Introduction to the Lectionary*, the purpose of the *profession of faith* is "that the assembled congregation may respond and give assent to the word of God heard in the readings and through the homily" (29). With one voice the body of Christ affirms that faith which is born of the word of God.

Also, inspired by the word proclaimed and preached, the faithful *offer prayers.* Having been formed more perfectly into the body of Christ by the word of God, the Church takes up Christ's work of interceding for the world. In light of the particular focus provided by the word voiced and interpreted, the assembly prays for the needs of the universal Church, for the local community, for the salvation of the world, for those who are suffering, and for other particular concerns that emerge from the interfacing of the word of God with local and world events. The work of interceding for the world in union with Christ is the perfect conclusion to the Liturgy of the Word.

Together, the Profession of Faith and the Prayer of the Faithful also serve as a fitting transition to the Liturgy of the Eucharist. When the assembly recites the creed, it calls to mind those mysteries of faith that will be celebrated in the Eucharist. And in offering intercessions, the community actually takes up the giving of itself for the sake of others that finds its completion in the eucharistic sacrifice.

OPENING TO THE JOY

To know that God is present and is ready to speak to us in ways that will renew, nourish, and equip us should fill us with a sense of joyful anticipation as we enter into the Liturgy of the Word. However, to receive the full benefit of this part of the liturgy we need to be prepared.

Preparing for the Proclamation

If we are going to be prepared to receive God's word it helps to know a little about why the particular readings we will be hearing are proclaimed. We should know that the readings are proclaimed from a Lectionary, that is, the Church's book of readings. (*Lectio* is simply the Latin word for reading.) The readings are taken from the Bible and are collected into books used for liturgical services primarily for the sake of convenience. In some cases the readings have been edited, usually meaning that some verses are left out in order to make the reading more immediately comprehensible for the hearers.

The principles guiding the choice of texts for Sundays are quite simple. In order to open up the riches of the entire Bible to God's people, each Sunday's liturgy includes three readings and a psalm. A reading is taken from the Old Testament (except during the season of Easter when the readings are taken from Acts), accompanied by a psalm that reflects in some way the meaning of the first reading. A second reading is taken from the New Testament Epistles. Then a passage from the Gospels completes the complement of readings.

Since we believe that the Old Testament finds its fulfillment in God's revelation in Christ, the Old

Testament text does not stand on its own. It is chosen because it is related in some way to the Gospel that will be proclaimed. The Epistle, itself being an expounding on some aspect of God's revelation in Christ, is chosen independently of the Gospel reading. During the seasons of the Church year that have particular thematic emphases—Advent, Christmas, Lent and Easter—readings are chosen that reflect those seasonal themes. During Ordinary Time, the Gospel is read continuously or semi-continuously, meaning that the next Sunday takes up from where the last Sunday left off, or close to it. The same is true of the Epistle reading. The readings are on a three-year-cycle (A,B,C), meaning that the same readings are read every third year.

Why is it important to know this about the readings? For one thing, the great amount of Scripture that is read over the course of three years speaks to us of the rich treasure that we have in sacred Scripture. Our reading from the whole of Scripture, including the Old Testament, is a living testimony to our belief that "all scripture is inspired by God and is useful for reproof, for correction, and for training in righteousness, so that everyone who belongs to God may be proficient for every good work" (2 Tm 3:16-17). And the particular importance given to the Gospel bears witness to our belief that Christ himself is the Word made flesh, the most perfect revelation of God. It is God's revelation in Christ that brings the rest of God's revelation into focus. Moreover, we believe that it is by sharing in the dying and rising of Christ that we are saved. So our liturgy is Christ-centered, something that is clearly reflected in the selection of the readings that are proclaimed each Sunday.

The Christ-centered nature of the liturgy is also reflected in the way we do the readings. The readings from the Old Testament and Epistles are each concluded with the pronouncement, "The word of the Lord." And in each case the people respond, "Thanks be to God." And we are truly thankful that God speaks to us through these inspired texts. But the Gospel is accompanied with words and actions that identify it as being the high point of the Liturgy of the Word. There may be a special book containing only the Gospel readings that is taken in procession from the altar to the ambo, sometimes accompanied by candles and incense. The people stand and sing an acclamation in praise of Christ, who is coming among us to speak a word of life. And following the Gospel proclamation, again the people join in acclamation: "Praise to you, Lord Jesus Christ!" To understand the significance of these words and actions is to know that we have great reason to be joyful in the Liturgy of the Word.

Yet while this general background helps us to understand why particular Scriptures are proclaimed in each Sunday's liturgy, it does not contribute much to our understanding of what the Scriptures *mean*. What will help us most in this regard is to actually study the readings for the upcoming Sunday in preparation for hearing them proclaimed in the liturgy. In the parish I serve we have a group that meets every Wednesday evening to discuss the readings for the upcoming Sunday. This sharing of insights gained from study and prayerful reading, along with whatever greater understanding emerges as we discuss the texts, is excellent preparation for the Liturgy of the Word.

I have often heard the participants speak of what a difference this makes in the actual hearing of the readings proclaimed in the liturgy. For one thing, the words are familiar. We don't have to mull over the meaning of particular words while the lector continues reading, leaving us behind scrambling through our mental dictionary. Also, we are ready for any diversions in a text, such as references to other Scripture passages or events in history with which we are unacquainted. Having studied the text beforehand, it is easier to stick with the text and listen with understanding. I often see the people who participate in our study group nodding or registering a smile of recognition as the reading is being proclaimed. They are definitely engaged in this part of the liturgy in a way that many are not. In this regard, a little advance preparation goes a long way. While it may not be possible for everyone to participate in such a group experience, it is possible for most of us to spend some time prayerfully reflecting on the next Sunday's readings, perhaps with the help of a study guide. (We have provided a small list of helpful resources at the back of this book.) Devoting a small amount of time to this each week will reap great benefits.

Focusing Our Attention

Studying the texts beforehand helps to focus our attention during the Liturgy of the Word. But for many of us, even with this advance preparation, being attentive during the readings still is something of a struggle. Often there are lots of distractions, both internal and external. To quiet the internal clutter it helps to offer a little silent prayer as the readers move to the ambo, asking God to assist them in proclaiming the word and to help us truly listen to what God has to say. Calling to mind that God himself speaks to us through the readings and that Christ himself is present, addressing us in the proclaiming of the Gospel definitely helps to focus our attention!

The external distractions may be more difficult to handle. Squirming babies, coughing pew mates, beeping watches and cell phones can certainly draw one's attention away from the lector. It is up to the parish community to find ways to lessen such distractions, by providing a nursery for infants and by occasionally addressing the matter of etiquette for the Sunday assembly in bulletin articles and pulpit announcements.

However, such distractions are bound to happen. When they do, it is important that we do not throw fuel on the fire by starting to talk to our pew mates about the distraction while the reader is courageously trying to continue, or by laughing at or engaging in pew play with children who are keeping people from focusing on the word of God. Such shenanigans will only insure that the distractions will continue. And if it is our children that are doing the distracting, then we must be considerate enough to remove them from the assembly until we can get them under control. When we begin to think that making a screaming child sit through Mass is more important than the community being able to focus on the God who is present and speaking through the readings, then we have definitely lost sight of the bigger picture! And if we are not the one causing the distraction, after realizing that we have been distracted, we must remember who is speaking to us and do our best to block out everything else.

Of course, this becomes even more difficult when the one doing the distracting is the lector. While it is the Church's responsibility to call forth lectors who have the necessary gifts and to provide them with sufficient training to serve well in this important ministry, sometimes things don't quite happen the way they should. Either someone is lectoring who really shouldn't be or the lector is just having a bad day. Perhaps he was in a hurry and forgot to comb his hair and a large clump is sticking up in some comical formation. Perhaps she didn't look in the mirror and her collar is half turned under. Perhaps he hasn't taken the time to prepare and makes some hilarious blunder like reading "flaming brassiere" when the text says "flaming brazier." (I've witnessed this very thing more than once!) Perhaps she is simply stumbling over words, mispronouncing and improperly inflecting as if suddenly English has become a foreign tongue. As members of the liturgical assembly, we will experience such things from time to time.

So how can we be attentive to the word when the one proclaiming it is the main distraction? To be quite honest, at times it is quite impossible without some special gift of grace. This is one reason why it is so important to study the readings before coming to the Sunday assembly. If we can't focus on the immediate proclamation, at least we have our own reading of the text to fall back on.

Also, at times we may have to be prepared to alter our approach to listening. Normally, it is best to look directly at the lector during the proclaiming of the readings. After all, a significant aspect of the awesome mystery unfolding here is that God's word comes through a particular human's speaking. Also, it helps the reader do a better job, since it is most encouraging to look out at people who actually seem to be paying attention. However, at times, especially if the lector's appearance is distracting, it may only be possible to focus on the word by focusing one's eyes on something other than the lector or by actually closing them. It may be possible to avoid this last resort by praying for lectors as they move to the ambo and by reminding our-selves that God intends to address us through this per-son's proclamation. If we do this little prayerful work in anticipation of the readings it may actually serve to rivet our attention, creating in us an eagerness to see how God will speak uniquely to us through a particular lector.

Responding Now and Later

All that I have said about focusing our attention on the reading also applies to the preaching. Perhaps even more than with the reading, some advance study of the texts will help us be attentive to the preaching. Those who participate in our weekly study of the Sunday readings in the parish are always eager to see how our discussions will connect with my homily. At times the connection will be obvious. In fact, they may even find that particular insights they offered during our meeting have been incorporated into the homily. Or, occasionally, they may be surprised to hear me say-ing certain things that weren't touched upon in our group discussion at all. Whether it is done as part of a group or not, such advance consideration of a text does increase our level of interest and readiness to be attentive.

Also, it helps both the preacher and the assembly if some kind of immediate feedback is given during the preaching. Even more than with the reading, it is important to look at the one preaching because the homily is intended to be a form of personal address. Preachers need our feedback if they are to continue to be excited about what they are doing. And we need to be involved with the preaching ourselves if we are to get the most out of it. A smile, a nod of the head, a look of genuine concern, a quiet but obvious "amen" or the silent clapping of hands (and in places where it will not disturb the faithful too much, with more audible and visible gestures) will definitely increase our attentiveness.

Another thing that will help maintain our focus during the preaching is if we listen with the intention of giving the preacher some significant response following the liturgy. What will we say to the homilist when we shake hands following the liturgy? Were we moved, challenged, disturbed, or delighted by a particular thing that was said? Do we have a word for the preacher that came to us through the preaching? Our intention to respond to the homily in some way that will benefit the preacher will not only contribute to the future effectiveness of his preaching, but it will also contribute to our attentiveness during the preaching.

Understanding What We Profess

As noted previously, hearing the word of God should lead to a profession of faith. But since our profession of faith following the homily is a ritualized response, if it is to be a genuine response then we must have some clear sense of the meaning of what we

are saying. Part of this is determined by our attentiveness to the word that has been proclaimed. If we have
listened well to the God who has been speaking to us
through the ministers of the word, we will certainly
have some understanding of the faith we profess. The
proclaiming and preaching of the word will have illu-
minated it. As we join in the communal recitation of
the creed, we should seek to be aware of the points of
connection between what we have heard, what we are
now speaking, and the lives we are living. It certainly
increases our level of participation in the profession of
faith when we are able to recognize that what we are
professing has something to do with us. In this way the
living word enlivens our faith.

Of course, it is a bit easier to make these connections if, outside of Mass, we take some time to learn
more about the various faith statements we make in
the creed. Participating in adult education opportuni-
ties in the parish that are intended to develop our
understanding of the faith can be most helpful in this
regard. Also, there are many books and videos available on all aspects of our faith that can be used for private study. For many people, the *Catechism of the
Catholic Church* is an excellent resource for develop-
ing a greater understanding of the faith we profess.
Devoting a little time to this kind of personal enrich-
ment will enhance our engagement in the Liturgy of
the Word immensely and will add to the enthusiasm
with which we profess our faith.

Fully Conscious of What We Pray

In a similar vein, to participate fully in the prayers we offer in response to the word, it helps to make conscious connections between the word we have heard and the intentions being voiced. This deepens our sense of the significance of the Church's intercessions. It also helps us to participate more fully in the Prayer of the Faithful in the Sunday liturgy if we are faithful in prayer throughout the week. If intercessory prayer is a regular part of our life, then we will be able to enter into it much more naturally and effectively during the liturgy. As we take time regularly to call to mind the suffering of God's people, as we reflect upon the fervent hopes and aspirations of those who yearn for the triumph of goodness, we cannot help but be moved to pray. And our daily prayers for the needs of the Church and the world, for divine assistance with all worthwhile activities and causes, prepares us to be fully conscious of what we pray for in the general intercessions of the liturgy. In this way, our response to each petition will be more than a detached and formal exercise in liturgical convention. When we embrace such praying as an essential part of who we are as members of the body of Christ, our participation in the Prayer of the Faithful truly becomes a heartfelt offering to the Father of things that concern us deeply.

QUESTIONS FOR REFECTION

1. Do you remember the first time you listened to the Word of God and heard God speak to your heart: how did it change you?

2. Identify the hopeful or healing word of God that was entrusted to you to pass on to another this week.

3. Which activities of your life would change, and how would they change, if you were to live more fully from the Word of God?

4. How much time do you spend each week with the Sunday readings in preparation for their proclamation at Mass?

5. As the Body of Christ, the Church, we pray the Prayer of the Faithful. How is the concern for all creation expressed in this prayer reflected in your personal prayer life?

Chapter 4

THE JOY OF MAKING EUCHARIST

OUR REASON FOR JOY

"When are we eating?" This is definitely an important question at our house. Gathering those who live in our house around the supper table for as many meals as possible is a priority for me. However, as with most other families, the demands of work, school, athletics, clubs and organizations has made it increasingly difficult for the whole family to be together every day for dinner. Undoubtedly, something important has been lost in the diminished frequency with which we are all together for meals.

Perhaps the upside of all this is that family meals on special days have taken on a greater significance. Holidays and holy days, birthdays and anniversaries have become essential gathering times for us. On such days our grown children usually find a way to make it home, while those still at home know that the usual social schedule must be put aside. Of course, this coming together involves something of a sacrifice for everyone—the sacrifice of making a long car ride, surrendering fun time with friends, laboring over a stove for much longer than usual, or setting aside some important piece of work that is begging attention. We make such sacrifices because we know that our being together is worth it. These sacrifices are "meaning-full."

Our coming together on special days is often quite relaxed. We may play games, watch sporting events on television, nap, take a walk around the neighborhood, go shopping, or watch a movie—all done quite spontaneously. We may split up into little groups that involve themselves in various activities of mutual interest. But the one thing that always happens, the main event for which everyone has come and in which participation is absolutely non-negotiable is the family meal. So on these days the question, "When is dinner?" is fundamental. For we all know that while everything else we do helps us to reconnect and strengthen our family ties, it is the sharing of the meal that is the real experience of communion. It is here that our life together as family is remembered, renewed, and celebrated in a way most focused and full. There is no distance or activity separating us and taking our attention away from one another. In this meal event, we are family in a way we seldom are at any other time.

At such times sharing our favorite foods is more than just an enticement for getting everyone together. The food is itself the primary sign that our gathering is truly special. Turkey, stuffing, homemade cranberry

relish, fresh rolls right out of the oven, mashed pota-
toes, and pumpkin pie are not incidental to our family's
Thanksgiving Day meal. In a real sense, it is this particular food that makes this a Damico family
Thanksgiving. In the same way, it would not be a
Damico family celebration of our son Christopher's
birthday without frozen peanut butter dessert. It's
Chris's favorite. The food is part of the meaning of the
meal.

As the food connects us to the life we have shared
as a family, it naturally leads to a remembering of significant moments in our common life. Our various
conversations *before* mealtime often are centered on
recent developments in our lives. They help us come to
a better sense of the current condition of our lives, of
the various joys and challenges we are experiencing at
the present moment. But the sharing of those favorite
foods that have always been part of our life together
tends to move us into a more historic kind of remembering. We find ourselves talking about all those special events that have become part of our family lore.
For instance, it wouldn't be a meal celebrating our
anniversary without the telling of stories about our
wedding. Though we have told them many times, it is
expected that Mary and I will recount some of the
most memorable details of that blessed event: where it
happened, who was in the wedding party, who read
and spoke, how we wrote and memorized our vows,
how it was so hot that the maid of honor passed out,

how Mary was stopped dead in her tracks when the recessional began because the maid of honor was standing on her train, and how her brothers put limburger cheese under the hood of our car to make our get away one we would remember for an odorously long time.

Each special meal has a certain standard group of stories attached that usually opens up into a wider remembering of special moments shared. We share them because these stories help define us. They help us to understand what it means to be the Damico family and why our gathering for a particular meal is so special. As we share stories, we laugh together, we express astonishment, we revisit moments of calamity and conquest, and we speak fondly of those who have played important roles in our family saga. In the process we come to a renewed sense of how our life together has been a source of blessing.

This remembering, then, leads to a sense of thanksgiving. It is implicit in the what and the how of our sharing. Sometimes it is expressed explicitly with comments like: "That was one of the best times I ever had," "We wouldn't be here today if she hadn't come along when she did," or "God was really with us that time!" Responses of "You're not kidding," or even an occasional "amen" affirm these expressions of gratitude.

As we share in this meal we are nourished by something more than just the food. In such moments we become present to one another in a way that we usually are not. And we draw strength from our being together in this way. We are nourished by our shared presence and by the remembrance of how our lives are enriched by our connectedness. Actually, something mysterious happens here that is beyond analyzing. We find ourselves being drawn into moments of loving communion that are sweet and that move us beyond the realm of our ordinary experiences of one another, uniting us deeply in a way that breaches the bounds of time and space. They are moments that cannot be explained but only savored.

These "meaning-full" moments often lead to the anticipation of things to come, future happenings that promise to bring the family together in new and even more wonderful ways. Weddings, the birth of grand-children, and landmark anniversaries are spoken of with genuine excitement. In the joy of our current coming together we are led to look forward to gatherings that will be more joyful still.

It should be no surprise that such meaningful moments involve a meal. After all, as my grandmother used to say whenever we visited her, "You've gotta eat." Because it is something we all have to do, it can engage the participation of an entire community. Such a significant and all-inclusive event is the perfect context for meaningful exchange, the kind of exchange that defines a community's identity and strengthens it.

So it is no accident that the most meaningful event in Hebrew history involved the sharing of a meal.

There is no clearer testimony to the significance of meals as a locus for meaning than what is provided in the story of the Exodus. The God who called the Hebrew people into existence and promised to be their God forever had responded to their cries for deliverance from Egyptian bondage. And with mighty signs and great wonders, he engineered their salvation. But even before the blessed event occurred, God instituted a meal in celebration of it.

The Lord said to Moses and Aaron in the land of Egypt: . . . Tell the whole congregation of Israel that on the tenth of this month they are to take a lamb for each family, a lamb for each household. If a household is too small for a whole lamb, it shall join its closest neighbor in obtaining one; the lamb shall be divided in proportion to the number of people who eat of it. Your lamb shall be without blemish, a year-old-male; you may take it from the sheep or from the goats. You shall keep it until the fourteenth day of this month; then the whole assembled congregation of Israel shall slaughter it at twilight. They shall take some of the blood and put it on the two doorposts and the lintel of the houses in which they eat it. They shall eat the lamb that same night; they shall eat it roasted over the fire with unleavened bread and bitter herbs. . . . You shall let none of it remain until the morning; anything that remains until the morning you shall burn. This is how you shall eat it: your loins girded, your sandals on your feet, and your staff in your hand; and you shall eat it hurriedly. It is the passover of the Lord. . . . This day shall be a day of remembrance for you. You shall celebrate it as a festival to the LORD; throughout your generations you shall observe it as a perpetual ordinance" (Ex 12:1-11,14).

Obviously, this meal is no ordinary meal. It is intended to be "meaning-full." Nor is it something intended to be celebrated only once. Because the deliverance of the Hebrews was the defining event of their existence as a people whose savior is the Lord, this Passover meal is to be celebrated in a similar fashion each year for as long as this people exists. This meal, that initially provided the necessary physical nourishment for a strenuous journey, is also intended to provide the spiritual strength and communal connections that will sustain them throughout history.

Knowing the significance of meals for God's people, and of the Passover meal in particular, Jesus chose this as the perfect setting to announce the great work of salvation that would establish the freedom of his followers forever. As a prelude to his death and resurrection, Jesus instituted a meal that would provide for a perpetual engagement in its meaning.

The Passover meal was the perfect context. But since the salvation Jesus was preparing to effect for us would be even greater than the deliverance of the Hebrews from bondage to earthly oppression, he had to expand upon the original symbols. He added a new layer of meaning to this ancient meal. In this new celebration Jesus focused on the elements of bread and wine. And he did it in a way that identified himself with these central symbols of salvation. In the Gospel we are told that, "While they were eating, Jesus took a loaf of bread, and after blessing it he broke it, gave it to the disciples, and said, 'Take, eat; this is my body.' Then he took a cup, and after giving thanks he gave it to them, saying, 'Drink from it, all of you; for this is my blood of the covenant, which is poured out for many for the forgiveness of sins'" (Mt 26:26-28).

Of course, bread and wine always had been important elements in the Passover meal. But Jesus chose to make them the central symbols of the meal his followers were to share in memory of him. In doing this, he was simplifying and focusing. Bread and wine were basic to the lives of his people. So these elements were "meaning-full."

Without bread and wine, there could be no life. To know this also is to know that there can be no life without *sacrifice*. Even the wheat and grapes necessary to make them must give up their lives, being harvested for the purpose of becoming food and drink. Their being made into bread and wine requires a sacrifice of time and effort on the part of those who process them. And their being served as food is certainly a sacrificial action. Bread must be broken and given, wine must be poured and shared. By identifying himself with bread and wine Jesus reveals to us that his sacrifice is essential for our coming to full and eternal life in the kingdom. It is the breaking of his body and the pouring out of his blood for us that makes salvation possible.

And how does one come to share in the salvation made possible by the sacrifice of Christ? This, too, is to be discovered in Jesus' use of bread and wine. Among his people, bread was the basic foodstuff for the nourishing of the body. Bread is what ensured the existence of God's people. Wine is what enlivened their spirit. It's no accident that we call such beverages "spirits." They have a way of lifting us out of the mundane in a way that invigorates and liberates. By identifying himself with bread and wine Jesus was saying that he is the fundamental source of nourishment for his people. It is by feeding on him, that is, by taking him into our lives and drawing life from him that we will have what we need to live eternally in God's kingdom. And it is by drinking him in, by allowing him to inspirit us, transforming us with his life-giving presence that we will be able to enter fully into the dynamic life of that kingdom.

Quite remarkably, Jesus says that those who share in this meal can do this quite literally. Of the bread, he says, "this is my body" and of the wine, "this is my blood." In other words, before he transforms us, he transforms the bread and the wine. He unites himself to them, changing them into gifts of his *presence.* This is essential to our understanding of what Jesus does for us in this sacred meal. Bread and wine cannot save us. We can only transcend the limitations of our mortal lives by receiving a share in the divine life. So in this meal Jesus gives us what we need. He becomes bread and wine for us. He allows us to take him into ourselves and to draw life from his divine presence.

This means that Jesus' command, "Do this in *remembrance* of me" (Lk 22:19), demands something more of us than what we normally think of as remembering. Usually, we understand the remembrance of something to mean thinking about something that happened in the past as simply that, a past event. However, this is not Jesus' meaning. If, in fact, he is commanding us to do something that makes him present to us, he must be using the word remembrance in another way. He must be speaking of the way of remembering that has been connected to the celebration of the Passover from its institution. Those who celebrate the Passover are not simply to think of it as a past event that didn't involve them personally. Rather they are to remember the liberation of their people by entering into that saving mystery *now*. To enter into the Passover meal rightly is to become one of the people who are being delivered by the saving power of God. In this way of remembering, one recalls the saving actions of God as one participating in them. So to share in the meal Jesus commands us to celebrate in remembrance of him is to enter here and now into the salvation God has achieved for us through the dying and rising of his Son.

Remembering in this way will naturally, and quite powerfully, move us to *thanksgiving*. For we know that the salvation we have in Christ is totally unmerited. It comes as pure gift of love. And this gift was purchased at a great price—Jesus' suffering and death. Thanksgiving, then, is the spirit that pervades the celebration of this meal. In fact, the word we most often use to speak of our sharing in this sacred meal is *eucharist*, which is the English equivalent of the New Testament Greek *eucharistia*, and means, quite literally, "thanksgiving."

Another reason Jesus chose a meal for keeping the remembrance of his saving sacrifice is that meals establish *community*. In the sharing of this meal, we become one body. As St. Paul says, "The cup of blessing that we bless, is it not a sharing in the blood of Christ? The bread that we break, is it not a sharing in the body of Christ? Because there is one bread, we who are many are one body, for we all partake of the one bread" (1 Cor 10:16-17). What Paul is saying is that a communion is established between us that is more than sentimental. It is organic. As we come to share in Christ's life through the Eucharist, we are necessarily and substantially united to one another. This is what it means to speak of the Eucharist as a sacrament of initiation. It brings us into full communion with those who are members of the one body of Christ.

In addition to binding us together with all who share in this meal of bread and wine, our communion with

Christ also defines what our life together must be like. It is to be a life given in loving *service.* As Christ gives his life for the salvation of God's people, so we must give ours. So important is this aspect of eucharistic understanding to the evangelist John that in his Gospel, instead of retelling the familiar story of the institution of the Eucharist, he focuses on what Jesus did following the meal. He tells us that when the supper was ended Jesus took a towel and washbasin and went around and washed his disciples' feet. It is in this action that John finds the key to understanding the Eucharist. Its meaning is communicated quite clearly to Peter: "Do you know what I have done to you? You call me Teacher and Lord—and you are right, for that is what I am. So if I, your Lord and Teacher, have washed your feet, you also ought to wash one another's feet. For I have set you an example, that you also should do as I have done to you" (Jn 13:12-15). John wants us to know that to share in the life of Jesus through participation in the Eucharist is to take upon ourselves the life of loving service.

One final aspect of the meal Jesus gives us to keep in remembrance of him is the *anticipation of the eternal banquet in God's kingdom.* Any meal involving those deeply united in partnership and purpose includes an element of looking forward to the completing or perfecting of what they have begun. This is especially true of those who eat and drink with Jesus. Such a gathering inevitably points to the future when the salvation we have already begun to experience will be fully realized, when God's reign will be established entirely and eternally. What we experience in the celebration of the Eucharist now is but a foretaste of the complete peace, joy, and abundance that we will share forever in God's kingdom. So even as we are filled, we find ourselves hungering for the more that awaits us in the promised land of heaven.

Though Jesus instituted the Eucharist in the context of the Passover meal, he obviously intended his disciples to share bread and wine together in memory of him more than once a year. According to Paul, Jesus instructed his disciples to celebrate the Eucharist every time they gathered together at table (1 Cor 11:25). This meal, which is our greatest source of identification and nourishment, is meant to be celebrated frequently. We need what it provides, and certainly more than once a year! That we share bread and wine together in remembrance of Jesus each Sunday when we gather at the Lord's house is rooted in the command of Jesus and makes the greatest of sense.

Obviously, we no longer celebrate the Eucharist in the context of a regular meal as the first Christians did. As the Church grew, the sharing of bread and wine in such a context became increasingly difficult. Guided by the Spirit, the Church came to realize that a structured liturgical setting was a better context for celebrating the Eucharist than was the more unruly environment of a community potluck. So the Eucharist was transformed into a ritual meal. However, this was done in such a way that all the meaning Jesus intended for this sacred meal has been preserved. *Sacrifice, presence, remembrance, thanksgiving, community, service, and anticipation* all emerge as significant elements in this "meaning-full" ritual meal. A brief overview of the eucharistic liturgy will help us come to a clearer sense of how this happens.

The Gifts We Offer

The Liturgy of the Eucharist begins with the *preparation of the gifts*. The sacrificial aspect of the Eucharist is immediately apparent as representative members of the faith community bring gifts of bread and wine to the altar. In the early Church, the sacrificial element of the preparation of the gifts was even more obvious than it is today. In addition to bread and wine, members of the assembly would present gifts of oil, candles, cheese, garden produce, and various other things that could be used in the worship of God and in service to the poor. Today parishes carry on this tradition by presenting the money offered for the work of the Church, along with the bread and wine. So the celebration of the Eucharist begins with the sacrificial offering of God's people.

Placed upon the altar, the gifts of bread and wine are prayerfully presented to the Lord. We bless the Lord for his goodness realized in having these gifts to offer and for his promise to transform them into a means of sharing in his divine life. The prayer spoken quietly by the priest when mixing a little water with the wine expresses well the hope that underlies the preparation of the gifts: "By the mystery of this water and wine, may we come to share in the divinity of Christ, who humbled himself to share in our humanity."

The *washing of the priest's hands* at this point, (once a necessity because of the many things received during the offertory that would have dirtied his hands), has become an important part of the preparation of the gifts. The quiet prayer he makes during this ritual washing, "Lord, wash away my iniquity, cleanse me of my sin" is not just a personal prayer. Rather, it reflects the sentiments of the entire assembly. It indicates an awareness that we are being offered along with the bread and wine—to become bearers of the divine life. And for this to happen we must be freed from our sins.

The sacrificial character of the eucharistic liturgy is brought to absolute clarity at the conclusion of the preparation of the gifts as the community prays that "the Lord will accept this sacrifice . . . for the praise and glory of his name, for our good and the good of all his Church."

In Great Thanksgiving

Following the preparation of the gifts, the Church enters into what has been known traditionally as "the Great Thanksgiving." As we enter into this prayer, in which the gifts presented are transformed into the body and blood of Christ, we recall the various ways that God has accomplished his saving work among his people throughout history. Elements of remembrance and thanksgiving are brought together in the *preface* to this prayer. Introducing the preface, the priest begins by reminding the people that the Lord is with them and calling them to turn to him wholeheartedly in praise and thanksgiving. The people respond by enthusiastically announcing their intention to do this very thing. The preface then goes on to state some of the reasons we have for giving God thanks and praise. There are a number of prefaces that may be used depending on the particular season, feast, scriptural emphasis, or occasion.

Fittingly the articulation of our cause for praise and thanksgiving leads to the joyful singing of the *Sanctus*. "Holy, holy, holy, Lord, God of power and might. Heaven and earth are full of your glory." This was the song sung by the angels in Isaiah's vision of the Lord in his temple (Is 6:1-3). As we take up this heavenly chorus, we are reminded of the great company of angels and saints with whom we are united in offering God praise and thanksgiving. The second part of the song, "Hosanna in the highest! Blessed is he who comes in the name of the Lord. Hosanna in the highest!" comes from the Gospel story of Jesus' entrance into Jerusalem (Mt 21:9). Here we begin to focus on the central reason for our praise and thanksgiving. Jesus is coming to share his divine presence with us. Blessed is he who comes in the name of the Lord!

Are Transformed

With some eagerness then, the priest continues by asking God to send his Spirit upon the gifts we have offered to make them holy. As the Spirit hovered over the waters and was active in the creating of the earth, so the Spirit is called down upon these gifts of the earth to effect a new creation.

Following this prayer, traditionally known as the *epiclesis,* the priest takes the bread and the wine and speaks the words of Christ over them, "Take this all of you and eat it. This is my body which will be given up for you." "Take this all of you and drink from it. For this is the cup of my blood, the blood of the new and everlasting covenant. It will be shed for you and for all so that sins may be forgiven. Do this in memory of me." We speak the words of Christ in the belief that, as in the proclamation of the Gospel, when his words are spoken in the assembly, Christ is present speaking to his people. And the word of Christ is effective, accomplishing what it signifies. Through Christ's speaking these words of consecration once again, our gifts of bread and wine are transformed into his body and blood.

Such a glorious happening surely calls for a response. So, following the *words of institution,* the assembly joins in the *memorial acclamation*. Together we proclaim the mystery of our faith, that through the dying and rising of Christ salvation has come to us—something we have experienced profoundly in the transforming of the gifts of bread and wine into his own life-giving presence. This proclamation of the saving activity of God in Christ leads into what is called the *anamnesis*, that is the *holy remembering* of how our salvation has been achieved in Christ. The priest recalls how Christ gave his life for us upon the cross and was raised up in glory. In this holy remembering we are taken up once again into this awesome reality of sacrifice and salvation. And we are filled with wonder by the knowledge that we are saved by this sharing in the dying and rising of Christ.

This holy remembering naturally leads to joyful *offering*. In thanksgiving for the salvation that has come to us in Christ, we offer the gifts that have been transformed upon the altar to the Father for the continuation of his saving work. And we offer more. We offer the gifts that have previously been transformed through the sacrament of baptism, that is, we offer ourselves. And all is offered as gift to the Father for the accomplishing of his work. Quite fittingly, then, as a sign of our eagerness to do what we have said, we actually take up this work right on the spot by offering *intercessions*. We pray for the Church, the world, and those who have died, that God's saving purposes may be accomplished for all.

The great eucharistic prayer then ends on the same note on which it began, with an expression of praise and thanksgiving. Only now, the blessed exchange of gifts has been completed. The bread and wine we offered has been transformed into the body and blood of Christ. The gifts of our own lives have been taken by God and united with the sacrifice of Christ for the salvation of the world. Heaven has united with earth in a way that brings new life to all creation through Christ from whom all good things come. And so the priest concludes the prayer with the joyous *doxology,* "Through him, with him, in him, in the unity of the Holy Spirit, all glory and honor is yours, Almighty Father, forever and ever."

And the assembly responds with a hearty, "Amen." Notice, I said "hearty." The "*amen*" is the appropriate response of the assembly. It is the assembly's way of saying "yes" to the prayer, of proclaiming its whole-hearted assent to all that has been said and done. Singing the "Amen" has a way of communicating the significance of this response in a way that a quick and quietly spoken "amen" does not. Thus, it is recommended that the Doxology and the Amen be sung whenever possible in the Sunday liturgy.

And Given to Us

Realizing that Christ is present upon the altar, offering himself to us under the form of bread and wine, we should be most eager to receive him. As an expression of this eagerness, *we pray the prayer that Jesus himself taught us.* We ask him to give us our daily bread. In other words, we ask for the nourishment we need to complete our journey into his kingdom, the gift of his own divine life that we receive in the Eucharist. We ask as people who know that receiving this gift requires something of us. Since it is the very nature of Christ to give himself on behalf of others, if we are to receive a share in his life, then we must be prepared to do the same. We cannot be in communion with Christ if we are not also in communion with those who are the members of his body.

So we exchange a *sign of peace.* This sign of peace is no small or incidental exercise. As we prepare to share in the sacrament of holy communion, we intentionally remove any barriers that may stand between us, offering one another a word and a gesture that proclaims we are at peace. Here we are making peace in the biblical sense of the term. We are establishing *shalom,* that is the kind of harmony and wholeness that God intends for creation. When we exchange peace, we are saying that there exists between us the kind of unity that typifies life in the kingdom.

It is only when this peace has been established among the body of Christ that we are prepared to receive the gifts of bread and wine. As the *bread is broken and the wine is poured* for distribution, the people sing the song of the *Lamb of God,* who takes away the sins of the world and grants us peace. The forgiveness of sins and the establishing of peace is something we have experienced profoundly in the eucharistic liturgy. And our singing of it increases our eagerness to come to the table of the Lord and to share fully in the holy communion that we already have begun to experience.

The priest's dropping of a little piece of bread into the cup of wine, called the *commingling*, is a sign of this full communion. In the early church, this little ritual was developed as a sign that a particular congregation was in communion with the whole Church. Pieces of consecrated bread were taken from the eucharistic celebration at the cathedral church to other churches in the vicinity and dropped in the chalice during their eucharistic celebrations. This expanded the sense of communion within the body of Christ in a marvelous way. It is helpful to remember this layer of meaning, as it definitely enriches our sense of being in communion with the whole body of Christ. However, in modern times, the emphasis of the commingling has been placed on our communion with Christ as he gives himself to us in the eucharistic species. The mingling of the bread with the wine is a sign that in both eucharistic species Christ is present whole and entire. While partaking of both the consecrated bread and wine is obviously a fuller symbolic participation in holy Communion, the commingling assures us that communion may be achieved fully even if only one of the sacred elements is received. This was a very important ritual gesture during those centuries when communicants did not receive regularly from the cup. In our own day, it is especially important for those who, because of some physical condition such as allergic reaction, can partake of only one of the sacred species. The commingling assures all who receive the Lord only under the form of bread or wine that their communion with him is in no way compromised.

When the consecrated bread and wine are prepared for distribution, the priest extends the *invitation to Communion*. Holding the sacred elements up before the people he announces, "This is the Lamb of God, who takes away the sins of the world, happy are those who are called to his supper." And the people respond, "Lord, I am not worthy to receive you, but only say the word and I shall be healed." This response to the invitation to share in the Lord's Supper expresses a humility appropriate for those who know that they are saved by grace alone and the eagerness of those who know that in Christ this grace has been offered to all who will receive it.

And this eager response is rewarded as God's gifts of bread and wine are distributed to the people. It is in this distribution of the sacred elements that we come to see the full mystery of the Holy Communion that is being celebrated. Here, the body of Christ is being given to the body of Christ by the body of Christ! Christ is present in the eucharistic elements, in those who administer them, and in those who receive them.

We see the many faces of Christ in the *eucharistic procession* as, one by one, the members of the assembly present themselves to those who joyfully share with them the bread of life and the cup of eternal salvation. We see the many hands of Christ as gifts of bread and wine are imparted and received.

Filling Us and Making Us One

As Communion is being distributed the church is filled with the presence of Christ in a most remarkable way. Perhaps a song is sung that heightens our sense of being in communion. Or perhaps the distribution of the holy gifts is done in silence, as together we enter into the awe and wonder of a mystery that is beyond words. What is important to realize is that this is no time to become overly self-focused, as though suddenly upon receiving Communion we have been transported out of the assembly into some private encounter with the Lord. While there is certainly room for personal devotion here, it is always within the context of the communal. Our awareness of being in communion with the assembly is part of our awareness of being in communion with Christ. Since Christ exists as a body and not just as an individual, we cannot be in full communion with Christ without being in communion with those who make up his body. This is why we do things that involve the entire community, like singing and praying, both during and following the distribution of the

Eucharist. To simply leave the church upon receiving Communion, as some still do, is to miss much of what the Communion received is all about. It is like sneaking out of a wedding banquet without offering a word of blessing to the bride and groom and their families. Of course, there may be a situation in which one has no choice but to do this. However, this is certainly not acceptable as standard practice.

After the Eucharist has been distributed and a time of communal silence has been observed by all, the presider brings the prayers of the people together audibly in a collect called the *prayer after Communion*. It is a prayer asking that the benefits of this Holy Communion will be realized fully by all who have shared in it. And it brings to our collective awareness the many reasons why our celebration of the Eucharist is a source of great joy.

OPENING TO THE JOY

While the celebration of the Eucharist is the climax of the Sunday liturgy, often there is much less intentional preparation for it than for the hearing of the word. Yet there are many ways in which we can prepare ourselves to enter more fully into the Liturgy of the Eucharist.

Immersing Ourselves in a Mystery

One thing that keeps people from sharing more deeply in the celebration of the Eucharist is the great mystery that lies at its center. How can Jesus become bread and wine? This is a common question among the followers of Jesus. For some, it is a point of monumental struggle. Their doubts lead to a half-hearted or even guilt-filled participation in the Eucharist. Others simply choose to ignore the issue and share in the Eucharist with a faith that is tepid at best. Full participation in the eucharistic banquet cannot be achieved by either a rejection of mystery or an evasion of it. Rather, it is by immersing ourselves in mystery that we prepare ourselves for enthusiastic and joyful participation in the Eucharist.

Perhaps it is best to begin by reflecting upon the mystery of our lives instead of immediately focusing upon the eucharistic mystery. After all, we are a bit better acquainted with the mystery we have been living, though there is certainly a profound connection between the mystery of our lives and the mystery of the Eucharist. If we are the least bit reflective, we cannot help but have a sense of the mystery of our own lives. I constantly find myself wondering as Mary did at the Annunciation, "How can this be?" As I experience the usual nervousness before presiding and preaching at a Mass, I find myself asking, "What is a person inclined to equally large doses of social anxiety and depression doing in this particular vocation?" On those days when

I am feeling totally without energy or enthusiasm and something kicks in, enabling me to preach or teach with vigor and a high degree of effectiveness, I find myself musing—"Where in the world did *that* come from?" From day to day I find myself pondering such things as: "Why do I love my wife?" "How is it that our children are so different?" "How do I explain the strange little happenings I have experienced at crucial moments that have opened doors or put up road-blocks?" "What do I make of an old man's experience of *seeing* a deceased relative soon before he died, or a dying woman's joyful announcement that she has been visited by the Blessed Mother?" The mystery of my very existence, how I manage to live from day to day, absolutely astounds me at times. And when I multiply this by the mystery of all those in whose lives I share but do not fully understand, I find that much of life is a mystery. This is something I have come to accept. In fact, it is something I celebrate. The mystery is what makes life fascinating and forever fresh.

The more we take time to immerse ourselves in the mysteries of our own lives, the more comfortable we will become with the mysteries of our faith. Knowing the wonderful complex of surprises that make up our own lives makes it much easier to accept and celebrate those great surprises that comprise God's saving actions throughout history. The central mysteries of the Christian faith—the Incarnation and the dying and rising of Jesus—through which God has given us a share in his divine life, will seem no less strange. But they will become increasingly believable. We will come to see that, as the angel Gabriel said to Mary, "Nothing is impossible with God." When we become well acquainted with the mystery of our own existence we will discover that the mystery of the Eucharist is consonant with the mystery of all life.

Remembering What God Has Done for Us

In the Eucharist we remember with great thanksgiving the major events in the history of salvation. To enter more fully into this great thanksgiving it helps to learn about those great events recalled in our eucharistic prayers. It is good to learn something about the high points of Hebrew history—creation, the saving of Noah and his family from the waters of the flood, God's covenant with Abraham and his descendants, the deliverance of God's people from Egyptian bondage, the conquest of the Promised Land, the establishing of the Davidic Kingdom, the sending of prophets, and the rebuilding of Jerusalem following the exile. We should certainly become acquainted with the high points in the history of the early Church—the life and ministry of Jesus, the sending of the Spirit, and the growth of the Church through the inspired work of missionaries and martyrs.

As we become more familiar with our salvation history, we will have stronger connections with the prayers and ritual actions of our eucharistic celebrations. They will come more fully alive for us. Our engagement in the eucharistic liturgy will be even greater if we take time to reflect upon our own personal salvation histories and relate them to the great stories of our faith tradition. What was *our* creation like? What was the setting of our coming into existence? What kinds of disasters have we survived? When did we first become aware of God's call to be one of his people? What obstacles has God helped us to overcome? How has God blessed us with family, possessions and livelihood? How did God bring us into his Church? What people have touched our lives and have helped us grow in faith?

I engaged in a reflection something like this recently while on my way to visit my father in Florida. I found myself deeply moved as I thought of the many ways he has helped me, provided for me, suffered for me, and nurtured me over the years. As I reflected on all he has done for me, my sense of anticipation at our coming meeting grew immensely. I was filled with feelings of love and appreciation as I completed the journey to my father's house. As a result, our time together was filled with a significance I had seldom experienced before. I was truly delighted to be with this man who had done so much for me. In the same way, devoting some reflection to all God has done for us will increase the joy we experience when we enter into the Liturgy of the Eucharist.

And Mindful of Our Current Needs

Of course, the more we become aware of all that God has done for us the more we may become aware of how little we have done for God. We may think of the many ways we are still held captive to sin, of our weakness in the face of temptation, of our failure to bear witness, of our lack of compassion and generosity, and of the various ways we have misrepresented the Christian life by our words and actions. In our remembrance of the many ways that God has enriched our lives we may find ourselves being overwhelmed by a sense of how much we need God to enrich us even more. We begin to long for the spiritual nourishment that God offers us in the Eucharist. We find ourselves hungering for what we need to grow into the likeness of his Son. For we know that we cannot be Christ for one another unless God's power is at work in us, as it is in him.

We Become Like Hungry Children

I was a chubby child. It was obvious to everyone that I was well provided for in the food department. Yet, while there was always plenty to eat at our house, I always found myself becoming exceedingly hungry on those days when my father went food shopping. My mouth watered as I thought of his arrival. I was there waiting when he came through the door. For on shopping days my dad always brought us some special treat. The eagerness of my greeting on those days must have given me the appearance of a baby bird in a nest, neck straining, with mouth wide open. "Feed me. Feed me. Give me something good to eat." My hunger for the tasty treasures to be brought forth from dad's shopping bag knew no shame.

When we become the least bit aware of the delightful gifts that God provides for us in the Eucharist, we will enter into its celebration like the hungry child I have just described. As we anticipate receiving the most wonderful of all foods, we will join eagerly in the chorus, "Blessed is he who comes in the name of the Lord." So it is important to take time before coming to Mass, and in those quiet moments provided in the liturgy to think of what it is that God is preparing to give us in the eucharistic banquet. If we do, we will approach this sacred meal with the joy and enthusiasm of hungry children who have just been invited to the table.

Learning to See Christ in One Another

Though I savored the treats my father brought home on shopping days, what made the experience even more delightful was being able to share it with others. My mother, grandmother, aunt, and sister were all there. And they enjoyed the special treats as much as I did. This communal sharing of the fruits of my father's kindness and generosity turned a brief moment of indulgence into a genuine celebration.

When we learn to recognize others in the assembly as family, as brothers and sisters in Christ who are sharing together the precious gifts of God, our joy in the celebration of the Eucharist is marvelously increased. While it is easy to turn the Eucharist into a private experience, to do so is to lose the grandness of it. The Eucharist is a banquet. We are eating and drinking with Jesus—the Jesus who gives himself to us as bread and wine, the Jesus who serves us, the Jesus who accompanies us to table.

To receive the full benefits of the Eucharist, it is necessary to open ourselves to this wonderful mystery. To accomplish this, rather than becoming overly intro-spective during the eucharistic liturgy, it is helpful to look around. As we look at those with whom we are sharing in this most wonderful of all meals we will do well to ponder the mystery of Christ's presence. Instead of focusing on the more mundane qualities of those who are processing with us to the altar, we can see through the eyes of faith God's beloved sons and daughters in whom the Spirit of Christ dwells. As we approach the minister of the Eucharist, we can remind ourselves that, through this member of his body, it is Christ himself who will be feeding us. The more we learn to view the members of the assembly in this way the more "meaning-full" and joyful our eucharistic cel-ebrations will be.

QUESTIONS FOR REFLECTION

1. Why did Jesus choose a meal for keeping the remembrance of his saving sacrifice?

2. What kind of "by example" training did the Lord provide for those who are his disciples?

3. The "Great Thanksgiving" prayer begins by stating some of the reasons we offer God thanks and praise. To enter more completely into this life-giving prayer, what current life events do we place before the Lord with grateful hearts?

4. How would you explain the difference between receiving Holy Communion and being in holy communion?

5. Does the mystery of faith have anything to do with the mysteries of your life?

Chapter 5

THE JOY OF BEING SENT FORTH

Our Reason for Joy

My grandmother Damico loved to have us come for a visit. Soon after we passed over the threshold of her house she would have us seated at table for a big spaghetti dinner. She encouraged us to eat and eat, and we were always happy to comply with her wishes. But, as difficult as it was on uncomfortably full stomachs, eventually we had to get up and engage in some physical activity just to keep from exploding or falling asleep. Before we left the table Grandma often said, "Now, Roddy, you're not going to leave without saying goodbye, are you?" Obviously, for her, the meal was not the end of our time together. There were some important things yet to be done and premature leaving would have left her feeling incomplete. And it would have left me without the good things she wanted to give me.

When we were preparing to leave Grandma Damico's house, she would always remind us of those important things happening in the family that needed our prayers or participation. Without fail, she would give my sister and me something to take with us, usually food or money. Then she would wish us a safe journey, exchange hugs and kisses with everyone, and stand there waving at us until we were out of sight. Something important would have been missing from our visit without the imparting of these final blessings. Her little concluding rituals seemed to bring a sense of completeness to our visit. We always left with smiles on our faces and with a sense that the bonds between us were strong.

So it is with the celebration of the liturgy. The concluding rites are not little ritual extras for those who choose to hang around after all the important things have been done. They are as essential to the assembly's gathering as were the little gestures at the end of those visits with Grandma Damico. In many parishes the concluding rites begin with announcements of special concerns or upcoming events. Like my grandmother's last minute reminders of important family matters, announcements seem appropriate at this time. While there are certainly other ways to communicate information, the sharing of a few special events and concerns that are important to our family of faith leaves us with an awareness that our connections with one another do not end when we go forth from the Lord's house. In fact, our sharing in the liturgy should increase our eagerness to be supportive of one another in the life of faith. Actually, announcements that are brief and well presented can be an effective preparation for the conclusion of the liturgy in which we are blessed and sent forth.

Being Filled with Blessings

The priest's *greeting* and *blessing* of the people mark the formal beginning of the concluding rite. Again, the priest reminds the people that the Lord is with them, and the people express their own faith in the Lord's abiding presence by reminding the priest of the same. Our response, "And also with you" functions like an "amen" only with the added dimension of relationship. We are a family of faith and it is important that we support one another. This is one of the reasons why it is important for the assembly to remain through the concluding rites. There is strength that comes from our being together for the special action that so fittingly concludes the liturgy.

Being thus supported by the community's affirmation of the Lord's presence, the priest prays that God will continue to enrich the lives of those who have participated in the liturgy. Usually this is in the form of a simple blessing, though on some Sundays of the Church year, it may be expanded into a three-fold blessing or a prayer over the people. As the priest speaks his words of blessing, he makes the sign of the cross over the people, while each one receives the blessing by making the sign of the cross over themselves. This sacred sign was first received when we were baptized into Christ. We made it at the beginning of the liturgy to remind us that we are members of the body of Christ. Now we make it again at the liturgy's end for the very same reason. It is in Christ that we have received God's blessings. And it is in Christ that we will be sent forth to carry on God's work.

This sending forth is of great importance. Without it we miss much of what the liturgy is really all about. In fact, "Mass," a word that we often use for the eucharistic liturgy, comes from the Latin word *missa,* which means *dismissal* or *sending forth.* To call the Sunday liturgy *the Mass* certainly tells us something about the purpose of this gathering. In the liturgy, we have come together as members of the body of Christ. We have been nourished by one another's presence, through the hearing of the word and through our sharing in the Eucharist. We have taken up the work of Christ, bearing witness to the greatness of God, interceding for the needs of the whole world, and offering ourselves in union with Christ for the world's salvation. But there is more to the work of Christ than this. And we know it.

We are not just members of the body of Christ for an hour on Sunday. What our being together for the Sunday liturgy does is to remind us of who we are *always.* And it provides us with the nourishment and support we need to be who we are, wherever we are. After all, it doesn't require perception beyond what most of us can muster to see that much still needs to be done in terms of reconciling the world to God. In those places where we live, learn, work, and play we often find ourselves in situations that do not reflect the love, peace, and justice that typifies life in the kingdom. Yet it is God's desire that all be brought into his kingdom. It was for this reason that Christ was sent into the world. And it is for this reason that we are sent forth as the body of Christ at the end of every liturgy.

The priest's dismissal, "The Mass is ended, go in peace," is basically code language that should be understood by all Christians. His words mean that the time of our gathering for liturgy has come to an end. It is now time to take up once again the saving work of Christ in the context of our daily lives. In other words, we aren't just *leaving* the Lord's house. We are being *sent forth* by the Lord. We are being dismissed from the assembly to be Christ's instruments of peace, servants of God who seek to establish everywhere the whole-ness and harmony of life in the kingdom. And since it is to establish Christ's peace that we are sent forth, we know that *he goes forth with us.*

In essence, at the end of every Mass we are dismissed in a manner similar to the first disciples who gathered in worship around the risen Lord. He said to them, "Go therefore and make disciples of all nations, baptizing them in the name of the Father and of the Son and of the Holy Spirit, and teaching them to obey everything that I have commanded you. And remember, I am with you always, to the end of the age" (Mt 28:19-20). As the echoing of this great commission, the dismissal at the end of Mass is too important to be missed. Besides, leaving before the dismissal leaves us without the joy of hearing that Christ thinks enough of us to entrust us with carrying on his work in the world.

It is this spirit of joy that should be reflected in the *recessional,* which is the final action of the liturgy. In terms of the structure of the Mass, the recessional provides a beautiful symmetry to the liturgy. The liturgy began with a procession that symbolically gathered the people around the altar. Now the liturgy concludes with a symbolic dispersing of the people from the altar into the world. This action makes it obvious where the power comes from for what we are being sent forth to do. The priest kisses the altar to begin this movement. Then, usually led by the cross, the servers and the priest move from the altar to the main entrance of the church, going out just the way they came in. Most often, this recessional is accompanied by the singing of a song that reflects the joyful dispersing of God's people to carry out the Lord's work. It is not necessary that the entire congregation remain in place for all the verses of this song. Since the recessing of the priest and servers is the symbolic beginning of the going forth of the people, the rest of the assembly should wait until they have made their movement through the church. Then, those in the assembly are free to follow, since this is what the recessional is all about. It is a mistaken notion to think that all must remain in place until the final word of the song is sung. After all, this is a *recessional.* It is for the purpose of recessing. In this regard, it does help if the recessional music is well known so people can continue singing as they go forth, without books in hand. This makes for a joyful movement and communicates the sense of dispersing that the liturgy intends.

OPENING TO THE JOY

Opening to the joy of the Concluding Rites is a matter of *appreciating the gifts received* and *resolving to make use of those gifts* as we go forth. It seems that the best time to do both is during the time between receiving Holy Communion and the Prayer after Communion. In those quiet moments of the liturgy it seems appropriate to reflect on what we have seen, heard, and done, and on the particular gifts we have received from the Lord in this liturgy to help us share life with him more fully. Such reflection cannot help but move us to joy and thanksgiving.

It will also create in us a desire to use the gifts we have received for the good of others. It will lead us to ask such questions as: What can I do with these gifts that will make a difference? Do I find in them a call to spend more time tending to the needs of my family? Do they inspire me to try to reach out to people at work in caring ways? Do they challenge me to address an issue of justice or morality that I have been avoiding? Do they push me to be more generous in sharing my resources with others? Do they invite me to spend more time praying for those in need? Of course, if it is to be of real value, such reflection must lead to resolution. We must resolve to do something specific in the coming week as those who have been gifted and sent forth to carry on the work of Christ. If we take the time to do this, we will find the dismissal to be a "meaning-full" moment in the liturgy. And the recessional will find us moving out with a spring in our step and a song in our heart.

QUESTIONS FOR REFLECTION

1. Is the Mass ended, or has it just begun?

2. Do we leave our treasures hanging in the pew in front of us or do we take them along to enable us to build a better world?

3. How do we bless each other and journey together into another week of living, loving, and giving?

4. Aware of your transformation through participation in the liturgy, how will you stretch and grow into a better appreciation of the gifts you have to offer and your ability to identify the needs of your brothers and sisters?

5. Name one way that your place of employment, school, home, city, will be a happier and holier place because of your presence this week.

POSTSCRIPT

As I come to the end of this little book I find myself thinking of those two disciples walking along the Road to Emmaus on the first Easter Sunday. They were discussing the things that had happened recently, things that had turned their world upside down. Jesus, whom they had thought to be the messiah, had been tortured and killed. His disciples were in hiding. Some of the women had been to the tomb only to find Jesus' body missing and to be greeted by mysterious messengers who said he was alive. They didn't know what to make of all this. Terribly confused and deeply discouraged, they were bereft of joy.

Then Jesus came along and walked with them. But they were prevented from recognizing him. This divine intervention was preparing them for an important revelation. After establishing a relationship with them, Jesus proclaimed to them the Scriptures. And he interpreted the Scriptures so his disciples could understand what they had to do with their present situation. As he did this, they were filled with a new energy and enthusiasm. So enlivened were they by his proclaiming and interpreting of the Scriptures that they begged him to stay with them for dinner. There, at table, he took bread, blessed it, broke it, and gave it to them. It was then that their eyes were opened fully and they recognized him. Then he vanished from their sight so there would be no confusion about what he was revealing to them.

What he was revealing to them was this: It was in their gathering with Jesus for the sharing of the word and for the breaking of the bread that his followers would find him. And this would always be a joyful and meaningful meeting. But they were not to linger there forever. As his disciples, they had things to do. However, the gathering with Jesus was absolutely essential, for it was here that they received what they needed to go on their way rejoicing and to do their work effectively.

Now, more than ever, we need to be reminded of the importance of our coming together with Jesus for the proclaiming of the word and for the celebration of the Eucharist. For the truth is that we find ourselves in terribly confusing and discouraging situations. Violence is all around us, posing a constant threat to the world's people. We are badly shaken at times by hurtful things that sometimes happen within the circle of Jesus' followers. Christians continue to be attacked by those who do not believe. And many of those who do believe seem to be hanging on by only a thread. In these days, as in all days, it is essential to remember where it is that Christ is always to be found—in the gathering of his people in the Lord's house for the proclaiming of Scripture and for the breaking of bread. It is here that our joy will be restored. It is here that we will find renewed enthusiasm for carrying on the saving work of Christ, as members of his body.

Yet this life-giving encounter with Christ in the liturgy is not automatic. The faithfulness and skill with which lectors, eucharistic ministers, musicians, preachers, ushers, greeters, and servers carry out their ministries can do much to open us to participation in this gracious mystery. (Hence the other books in this series as listed on p. 127.) But if we are to experience fully the joy of worshiping together, the most important ingredient is the sense of the entire assembly that what it does truly matters. We do not come together simply to *watch* others perform certain ministries that impart to us spiritual gifts. We are *involved* in the imparting. The active participation of each one present makes Christ more fully present. As each of us is enriched in this wonderful work of liturgy, we are enriching the lives of others and of the whole world. To know this is to know the joy of worshiping together.

BIBLIOGRAPHY

Chapter 1 - The Joy of Worshiping Together

Bernstein, Eleanor, CSJ., editor, *Liturgical Gestures, Objects.* A collection taken from *Assembly,* a publication of the Notre Dame Center for Pastoral Liturgy, 1995.

Huck, Gabe and Chinchar, Gerald T. *Liturgy with Style and Grace,* 3rd Edition. Chicago, IL: Liturgy Training Publications, 1998.

Huebsch, Bill and Thurmes, Paul. Vatican II in Plain English: *The Constitution on the Sacred Liturgy - Study Edition.* Allen, TX: Thomas More Publications, 1997.

Philippart, David. *Saving Signs, Wondrous Words.* Chicago, IL: Liturgy Training Publications, 1996.

Chapter 2 - The Joy of Gathering

Conners, Daniel. *Assembly.* From "I Like Being in Parish Ministry" Series. Mystic, CT: Twenty-Third Publications, 2001.

Gaeta, Francis X. *From Holy Hour to Happy Hour.* Totowa, NJ: Resurrection Press, 1996.

Mahony, Cardinal Roger, *Guide for Sunday Mass: Gather Faithfully Together.* Basics of Ministry Series. Chicago, IL: Liturgy Training Publications, 1998.

McGloin, Kevin. *What Every Catholic Needs to Know About the Mass.* San Jose, CA: Resource Publications, 2000.

Worship Office of the Archdiocese of Cincinnati. *We Gather in Christ: Our Identity as Assembly.* Chicago, IL: Liturgy Training Publications, 1996.

Chapter 3 - The Joy of Receiving a Life-Giving Word

Baisas, Bienvenido, OFM., Duffy, Rachel, F.C.J., etal. *Bible Diary* - combines 365 days of Bible readings and reflections with a daily planner and appointment book. Mahwah, NJ: Paulist Press, 2002.

Connell, Martin, *Guide to the Revised Lectionary.* Basics of Ministry Series. Chicago, IL: Liturgy Training Publications, 1998.

Zimmerman, C.PP.S. Joyce Ann, etal. *Living Liturgy.* Cycles A, B, C. Collegeville, MN: The Liturgical Press, 2000-2002.

Rosser, Aelrod. *A Word That Will Rouse Them.* Chicago, IL: Liturgy Training Publications, 2000.

Chapter 4 - The Joy of Making Eucharist

Emmanuel. Magazine of eucharistic spirituality. Published ten times a year by the Congregation of the Blessed Sacrament.

McCarron, Richard, *The Eucharistic Prayer At Sunday Mass.* Chicago, IL: Liturgy Training Publications, 1997.

Anderson, Frank, M.S.C., *Making the Eucharist Matter.* First published in the U.S. in 1999 by Ave Maria Press, Inc. by arrangement with John Garrarr Publishing, Mulgrave, Australia.

Chapter 5 - The Joy of Being Sent Forth

Rohr, Richard and with Feister, John Brookser, *Jesus' Plan For A New World: The Sermon on the Mount.* Cincinnati, OH: St. Anthony Messenger Press, 1996.

United States Conference of Catholic Bishops. *Everyday Christianity: To Hunger and Thirst for Justice.* Washington, DC: USCCB Publishing.

United States Conference of Catholic Bishops. *Communities of Salt and Light: Reflections on the Social Mission of the Parish.* Washington, DC: USCCB Publishing.

THE JOY OF MUSIC MINISTRY
John Michael Talbot

"I encourage every pastor, musician, parish staff member, . . . to read this book."
—Fr. Dale Fushek

No. RP145/04 ISBN 1-878718-63-0 $6.95

THE JOY OF BEING A LECTOR
Mitch Finley

". . . practical, full of useful suggestions on how to be a better lector."
—Fr. Joseph Champlin

No. RP123/04 ISBN 1-878718-57-6 $5.95
Also Available in Spanish: La Alegria De Ser Lector No. RPS 123/04 $5.95

THE JOY OF BEING A CATECHIST
Gloria Durka, Ph.D.

"Chock-full of suggestions both practical and spiritual for gaining or maintaining our visions . . . perfect end-of-year gift." —Religion Teachers Journal

No. RP520/04 ISBN 1-878718-27-4 $4.95
Also Available in Spanish: La Alegria De Ser Catequista RPS520/04 $4.95

THE JOY OF TEACHING
Joanmarie Smith, C.S.J.

". . . a lovely gift book for all proclaimers of the gospel." —Religion Teachers Journal
No. RP114/04 ISBN 1-878718-44-4 $5.95
Also Available in Spanish: La Alegria De Ser Educador—RPS114/04

THE JOY OF PREACHING
Fr. Rod Damico

"A gem . . . should be read by every deacon and candidate." —Deacon Jerry Wilson
No. RP142/04 ISBN 1-878718-61-4 $6.95

THE JOY OF BEING A EUCHARISTIC MINISTER
Mitch Finley

". . . provides insights meant to deepen one's relationship to the risen Christ."
—St. Anthony Messenger

No. RP010/04 ISBN 1-878718-45-2 $5.95
Also Available in Spanish: La Alegria De Ser Ministro De La Eucaristia—RPS010/04

THE JOY OF MARRIAGE PREPARATION
Tony Marinelli and Pat McDonough

". . . will benefit not only those who prepare couples for marriage, but also those couples who approach this sacrament." —Bishop Emeritus John R. McGann
No. RP148/04 ISBN 1-878718-64-9 $5.95

THE JOY OF USHERS AND HOSPITALITY MINISTERS
Sr. Gretchen Hailer, RSHM

". . . share ways to make your parish a place of Welcome and Thanksgiving."
No. RP328/04 ISBN 1-878718-60-6 $5.95

Additional Titles Published by Resurrection Press, a Catholic Book Publishing Imprint

A Rachel Rosary *Larry Kupferman*	$4.50
Blessings All Around *Dolores Leckey*	$8.95
Catholic Is Wonderful *Mitch Finley*	$4.95
Come, Celebrate Jesus! *Francis X. Gaeta*	$4.95
Days of Intense Emotion *Keeler/Moses*	$12.95
From Holy Hour to Happy Hour *Francis X. Gaeta*	$7.95
Healing through the Mass *Robert DeGrandis, SSJ*	$9.95
The Healing Rosary *Mike D.*	$5.95
Healing Your Grief *Ruthann Williams, OP*	$7.95
Healthy and Holy Under Stress *Muto, VanKaam*	$3.95
Heart Peace *Adolfo Quezada*	$9.95
Life, Love and Laughter *Jim Vlaun*	$7.95
Living Each Day by the Power of Faith *Barbara Ryan*	$8.95
The Joy of Being an Altar Server *Joseph M. Champlin*	$5.95
The Joy of Being a Catechist *Gloria Durka*	$4.95
The Joy of Being a Eucharistic Minister *Mitch Finley*	$5.95
The Joy of Marriage Preparation *McDonough*	$5.95
The Joy of Music Ministry *J. M. Talbot*	$6.95
The Joy of Preaching *Rod Damico*	$6.95
The Joy of Ushers *Gretchen Hailer*	$5.95
Lights in the Darkness *Ave Clark, O.P.*	$8.95
Loving Yourself for God's Sake *Adolfo Quezada*	$5.95
Mother Teresa *Eugene Palumbo*	$5.95
Our Grounds for Hope *Fulton J. Sheen*	$7.95
Personally Speaking *Jim Lisante*	$8.95
Practicing the Prayer of Presence *van Kaam/Muto*	$8.95
5-Minute Miracles *Linda Schubert*	$4.95
Season of New Beginnings *Mitch Finley*	$4.95
Season of Promises *Mitch Finley*	$4.95
Stay with Us *John Mullin, SJ*	$3.95
Surprising Mary *Mitch Finley*	$7.95
What He Did for Love *Francis X. Gaeta*	$5.95
You Are My Beloved *Mitch Finley*	$10.95
Your Sacred Story *Robert Lauder*	$6.95